DEMAND and Grace

The Sermon on the Mount

Demand and Grace
The Sermon on the Mount

Edwin K. Broadhead

SMYTH&HELWYS
PUBLISHING, INCORPORATED · MACON, GEORGIA

Smyth & Helwys Publishing, Inc.
6316 Peake Road
Macon, Georgia 31210-3960
1-800-747-3016
©1999 by Smyth & Helwys Publishing
All rights reserved.

Edwin K. Broadhead

Biblical quotations are the author's translation from the original Greek.

Library of Congress Cataloging-in-Publication Data

Broadhead, Edwin Keith, 1955-
  Demand and grace: the sermon on the mount/
  Edwin K. Broadhead.
    p.   cm.
  Includes bibliographical references.
  1. Sermon on the mount—Textbooks.
  2. Christian life—Baptist authors.
  I. Title.
  BT380.B755   1999
  226.9'06—dc21   99-14810
                             CIP
ISBN 978-1-57312-269-6

To

Frank and Evelyn Stagg

from whose words I have learned much

from whose deeds I have learned more

Contents

Preface	ix
Introduction	1
The Kingdom Lifestyle Matt 5:3-16	17
The Kingdom Lifestyle and Law Matt 5:17-48	29
The Kingdom Lifestyle and Worship Matt 6:1-34	45
The Kingdom Lifestyle and Others Matt 7:1-6	57
The Kingdom Lifestyle and Self Matt 7:7-27	63
Conclusion	77
The Sermon's Impact	83
Epilogue	109
Annotated Bibliography	111

Preface

This book is designed to lead readers through the lessons of the Sermon on the Mount. My own experiences with the Sermon go back to childhood memories of classical portraits of Jesus preaching from the mountainside. Piety was renewed and combined with scholarship when the Sermon became the focus of my honors studies in college. There I discovered the careful scholarship of Joachim Jeremias and the committed discipleship of Dietrich Bonhoeffer and Clarence Jordan. My love for the Sermon was deepened when I served as graduate fellow for Professor Frank Stagg during his lectures on the Sermon at the Southern Baptist Theological Seminary in Louisville, Kentucky. Given at the close of his career in the classroom, these lectures were undergirded by his lifelong commitment to the radical call of Jesus. Further studies in the Sermon were taken under Professor Hans Weder, my doctoral supervisor at the University of Zürich. During my time in Zürich, I gained new awareness of the story of the Swiss Brethren and the larger Anabaptist movement. My own views and commitments have been profoundly shaped by these sixteenth-century disciples of Jesus.

Now at last I stand in the position of gathering these lessons into a study guide. While this study represents the culmination of many years of reflection and the coalescing of many spheres of influence, it is not a finished task. My own journey with the Sermon continues, with many lessons yet to be learned and the task of discipleship not yet finished.

Two commitments guide this study. On the one hand stands an unswerving commitment to careful historical-critical study of the Scriptures. On the other hand stands an unwavering commitment to piety and practice. In the quest for life the pilgrim can afford to abandon neither wisdom nor faith. Some who are unaccustomed to critical reading of biblical texts may be discomforted by positions taken here, yet they represent, for the most part, a broad consensus reached over many years by a host of careful scholars. Others may be discomforted by the explicit concern for piety and practice, for the Sermon represents an invasion into the equilibrium of comfortable Christianity. We who have been shocked by the Sermon stand in good company, for these words were first received with amazement (7:28) and with no small degree of controversy (7:29). This pattern endures throughout history, and the Sermon continues to intrude into the comfortable settings of our lives. May those who use this work to explore anew the teachings of Jesus experience a similar discomfort, challenge, and calling.

Introduction

The Sermon on the Mount presents the most appealing ideals of Christian faith, but at the same time the Sermon provides the most stinging critique of Christian practice. Mahatma Gandhi, the Indian philosopher and activist, expressed both sides of this equation. Gandhi was attracted to Jesus through these teachings: "The message of Jesus, as I understand it, is contained in the *Sermon on the Mount*. . . . It is that *Sermon* which has endeared Jesus to me."[1] Gandhi also saw in the Sermon a radical critique of Christianity: "The message, to my mind, has suffered distortion in the West. . . . Much of what passes as Christianity is a negation of the *Sermon on the Mount*."[2] This study seeks to recover the ideals of Christian faith as presented in the Sermon on the Mount and to encourage individuals and communities to practice that faith.

Development

While most studies discuss the Sermon on the Mount as it is found in Matthew 5–7 of modern Bibles, the Sermon developed through an intriguing process and has played a decisive role in Christian history. A brief sketch of that development and use will aid our understanding of the Sermon.

The Sermon on the Mount has its origins in the teaching of Jesus. It certainly reflects various aspects of its milieu (Judaism within the Graeco-Roman world of the first century of the common era). It also speaks to the concerns of the Christian communities that arose after Jesus' death and resurrection. The influence of the Gospel writers can be seen at various points. Nonetheless the dynamic language and the radical claim at the core of the Sermon must be traced back to the prophetic activity of a single historical figure—Jesus of Nazareth. Matthew makes it clear that we are to hear in these words the very claim of Jesus upon our lives: "And it was when Jesus completed these words, the crowds were amazed at his teaching, for he was teaching them as one having authority and not as their scribes" (7:28-29).

If this message originates in the teaching of Jesus, how does it come to be a part of the tradition of the church and a portion of the Gospel of Matthew? Jesus was not a modern teacher who had access to numerous books and tools of communication. He apparently left no written records of his teaching. His instruction was given and remembered in the form of oral communication. Most scholars think this teaching was presented in Aramaic, the form of Hebrew spoken in Jesus' native region. The teaching of Jesus was given in short, colorful sayings and stories that employed images from common life (farmers, housewives, birds of the air, sheep of the field, and so forth). These sayings and stories would have an immediate impact upon the imagination of his hearers. Such lessons were easily remembered and repeated, and they would become the subject of later reflection.

The teachings found in the Sermon on the Mount were probably used often by the earliest followers of Jesus as they carried out their own ministry. As these early Christian prophets and teachers announced the message of Jesus (the Kingdom of God), they drew upon the words Jesus himself had taught them. This was probably true already of those disciples who were sent out to announce the Kingdom of God within Jesus' lifetime; they did so by repeating the words of Jesus. This pattern became even more important after the death and resurrection of Jesus. His ministry and his message were continued by those who remembered and repeated the teaching of Jesus.

At first this message was given to the people of Jesus' own region in their native tongue. As the message spread, interest in the teaching of Jesus arose among people who did not speak Aramaic. Since the most prominent language of Jesus' day was Greek, the teachings of Jesus were eventually translated into Greek for more widespread missionary activity. At the same time the teachings of Jesus were used to address specific questions and needs within the Christian experience. Consequently there arose the need for some type of organization and arrangement for the various stories and sayings.

It is very likely that some early followers translated the teachings of Jesus from Aramaic into Greek and organized this material to address the needs of their own time. Both the translation and the organization of this material represent strategies for evangelism; they intend to make the message of Jesus available and relevant to their own situation. Eventually this material emerged in written form. Thus, written collections that presented the teaching of Jesus in organized form most likely circulated within the early church and were used in their presentation of the gospel. Scholars sometimes refer to this material as the Sayings Tradition, as the *logia* (the Greek word for "sayings"), or as Q (perhaps from the German word *Quelle*, which means "source").

The Evangelists, or the writers of the Gospels, drew upon sources when they wrote the Gospels found in our New Testament. Because the Evangelists were probably writing some thirty-five to seventy years after the death and resurrection of Jesus, they would need to draw upon the traditions of the early church. Matthew and Luke drew more heavily upon the collected teachings of Jesus than did the other Gospels. While some of this teaching may have come to them as remembered oral tradition, they most certainly drew upon written collections of Jesus' teachings.

At many points scholars think that Matthew and Luke drew upon the same written document to record the words of Jesus. When they present the most famous sermon of Jesus, Luke and Matthew give much of the same material. At the same time there are some clear differences in the sermon found in Luke 6:17-49 and the one found in Matthew 5–7. Luke's version of this sermon has become known as the Sermon on the Plain, while Matthew's version is known as the Sermon on the Mount. Most scholars think that Luke 6:17-49 and Matthew 5–7 are two different versions of the same teaching. The most likely reconstruction is that this teaching was taken from various events in Jesus' ministry, remembered and collected within the early church, and then presented in different ways by the Evangelists to address the needs of their own communities.

Setting

Insight into the situation of Matthew's community will help us to understand the presentation of the Sermon in Matthew 5–7. Matthew's Gospel reveals a strong dependence upon the text of the Gospel of Mark. Since most scholars believe the Gospel of Mark was written about the time of the fall of the Jerusalem Temple (70 CE), the Gospel of Matthew likely comes from the period of 70-90 CE. Specific aspects of this era illuminate the text of the Sermon.

With the fall of the Temple, Judaism lost one of its major centers of identity and focus. The Saduccees, who were closely associated with the power of the Temple, lost their authority. The Zealots who resisted Roman rule were suppressed. The Essene community at Qumran was destroyed by the Romans. As a result, the authority to interpret and maintain Jewish traditions fell largely to the remaining Jewish party—the Pharisees.

The Pharisees were laypersons marked by their more progressive and studious commitment to teach and practice the traditions of Judaism. They sought to consolidate Jewish faith around two poles: the Torah (scriptures) of the Jewish people and the local synagogues where the teaching of Torah took place. Because Jerusalem had fallen, the center for this Pharisaic renewal movement was the city of Jamnia, located some twenty-five kilometers west of Jerusalem.

In addition to the Pharisees, another group of Jewish believers sought to consolidate and renew the heritage of Israel in the aftermath of the Temple's destruction. While Pharisees saw the work of God gathered around the interpretation of Torah in the synagogues, this alternate group sought to reinterpret Jewish tradition around their experience with Jesus of Nazareth, whom they proclaimed as the messiah who, following his execution, had been raised by God. The Christian community, and Matthew's community in particular, claimed that the story of Israel and its Law have their definitive interpretation in the teaching of Jesus.

In the beginning both Pharisees and Christians sought to implement their renewal movements through the synagogues in various cities and towns beyond Jerusalem. This effort led naturally to much debate and to various levels of conflict.³ It appears that leaders of the synagogues began to institute prayers that condemned the followers of Jesus. Since Christians could not repeat this curse, they were easily identified and ostracized through worship in the synagogue. This curse—and perhaps other events—led eventually to the separation of the Christian church and the Jewish synagogue.

Within this context of reform and schism, the burning issue was the question of who held the power to interpret and extend the heritage of God's people Israel. The Gospel of Matthew belongs precisely to this setting. Jewish Christians had lost the Temple and had been excluded from the synagogue. They were labeled as Jews who had abandoned the Law and become unfaithful to the God of Israel. Drawing upon traditions circulating among the followers of Jesus, Matthew presents a different claim.

For Matthew, the Christian community is guided by the Teacher Jesus, whose authority exceeds that of scribes and Pharisees. His words do not abandon the Law, but rather extend and fulfill it. Jesus does not abandon the way of God. Rather, he announces the presence of God's rule. Through his instruction believers are called to a higher righteousness than that the scribes and Pharisees practiced. In Jesus' instruction, believers are called to fulfill the Law. The worship life of Israel is renewed through Jesus' call to authentic worship—through deeds of mercy, prayer, fasting, and faithfulness to God. The righteousness demanded in the Old Testament is to be realized in the life of Jesus' followers. The purest and best of Israel's faith is reclaimed in the community of Jesus' disciples. Here the God of Israel is being experienced and honored as the Heavenly Parent. The long-awaited reign of God has become reality among the followers of Jesus.

Matthew constructs his Gospel with these goals in view. The result is a written narrative account of Jesus' life, death, and resurrection that employs early Christian traditions to speak to the specific needs of

Matthew's own time and his own community. At the heart of this programmatic story lies the Sermon on the Mount.

Impact

Whatever its process of development, the Church has always stood convinced of the authority of the Sermon for Christian faith and practice. The continuing impact of Jesus' teaching in the Sermon on the Mount can be traced through Christian history. Only a few examples can be cited here.

The teaching behind Matthew 5–7 may be at work in other portions of the New Testament. In particular the book of James (with its emphasis on true wisdom, blessings, the law, and faith that works) may represent a further use of this material. Beyond the pages of the New Testament the influence of the Sermon on the Mount was early and extensive.[4] The *Didache*, a book of Christian instruction dated from 90-120 CE, draws heavily upon the Sermon. Matthew 5–7 is quoted in numerous places, and the teachings of the Sermon are reinterpreted to address the needs of the churches of that day. The two ways of life and death are discussed, and the Lord's Prayer is cited.

The Sermon on the Mount was the most frequently cited text in the period of Christian history that preceded the Council of Nicea (325 CE). In addition to the *Didache*, the Sermon played an important role in the thought of Justin Martyr, Irenaeus, Tertullian, Origen, and others. The Sermon was important in the preaching of Chrysostom (about 345-357 CE), the primary representative of the Antioch school of interpretation. Augustine wrote a commentary on the Sermon on the Mount somewhere between 392 and 396 CE. While he interpreted the Sermon through his own philosophical view of the world, Augustine saw in the Sermon "all the precepts by which the Christian life is formed."[5] The Sermon remained influential around the time of the Middle Ages through the thought of Thomas Acquinas and Cornelius a Lapide.

The Protestant Reformation of the sixteenth century provided renewed interest in the Sermon on the Mount. While the Sermon played a key role in the thought of Martin Luther, Ulrich Zwingli, and John Calvin, the greatest emphasis on the Sermon was found among a radical group of reformers known as the Anabaptists. Though Anabaptists emerged at various places within Europe in the sixteenth century, their primary origin was among the followers of Zwingli in Zürich. Their central aim was to reestablish the patterns of the New Testament Church. While others sought to reform church and state together, the Anabaptists strove to establish a pure church that stood over against the state and its government. They believed the Kingdom of God was to be realized here and now upon the earth. Their guide for this program was a serious and literal reading of the Sermon on the Mount.[6]

The impact of the Sermon continues into modern times. The Protestant liberalism of the nineteenth and early twentieth centuries was concerned to recover and to implement the religion of Jesus himself, rather than the doctrines others developed about him. This emphasis upon the social ethics of Jesus is typified in the thought of Albrecht Ritschl (1822–1889), Adolf von Harnack (1851–1930), and Wilhelm Herrmann (b. 1846). The ethical teachings of Jesus in the Sermon stood at the center of this movement.

Others pursued social and political agendas based upon their reading of the Sermon on the Mount. Leo Tolstoy, the Russian novelist and social reformer, based his activity on a strict literal reading of the Sermon. The resistance by Leonhard Ragaz, a Swiss thinker, to the growing power of the wealthy in Europe emerged in part from his reflection upon the Sermon. Dietrich Bonhoeffer resisted the growing power of Nazism through his reading of the Sermon. Clarence Jordan employed the Sermon in his resistance to racism in the American South. The Sermon was the driving force behind the nonviolent resistance preached by Martin Luther King, Jr. The Sermon has received renewed attention among Jewish scholars in recent years, and it continues to play a central role in biblical scholarship.

While the Sermon has influenced various periods of thought, we cannot simply take over the ideas or the life of another generation. The Sermon must be interpreted, reflected upon, and acted upon in different ways for each new generation and circumstance. While we learn from the thought of those before us, we must ultimately read and act upon the Sermon within our own situation, within our own history. We turn now to some principles that might guide our interpretation.

Dangers of Interpretation

In reading the Sermon on the Mount there are some dangers to be avoided. First, we must avoid the temptation to see the Sermon as the ladder to perfection. Some have seen in the Sermon a new law that surpasses the Law of Moses in its strictness. They believe that perfection would be reached by those who could keep the demands of the Sermon. The danger in this view is that it creates a new legalism that depends upon extraordinary human efforts to achieve God's blessings. Only a few could hope to follow this path.

A second danger lies in the temptation to see the Sermon as an unreachable ideal. Some think the Sermon is God's way of pointing out our failures and reminding us of our need for God. The danger of this position is that it leads to despair and that by making the Sermon unattainable, it tends to make the Sermon irrelevant.

The tendency to see in the Sermon God's demands for someone else must be avoided. Some interpreters thought the Sermon was only for the first followers of Jesus. Others saw in it principles that could be followed only by the clergy or those having a religious vocation. Christians should not see the Sermon as a guide solely intended for spiritual matters, while living by secular standards in other realms of life.

We should avoid seeing the Sermon as God's instruction for another time. Some believe that Jesus' demands were only binding in the last days of the world. Others argue that the Sermon is relevant only for some other "dispensation" or period of history. Those who live in normal times would then be required to work out different patterns of conduct.

We must avoid the danger of reducing the demands of the Sermon to generalized principles applicable to any situation. Many have used this approach to soften the radical demands of the Sermon and to justify alternate patterns of conduct.

The Sermon should not be reduced to a personal piety that has no effect upon the life of the world about us, nor must we see the Sermon as a social agenda that has little impact upon our personal relationships and actions.

Finally, we must avoid interpretations that separate the Sermon from the culture in which we live. Conversely we must resist the temptation to so adapt the Sermon to our own culture that it loses its prophetic power.

Principles of Interpretation

How can we as modern readers interpret the Sermon on the Mount in a way that takes it seriously, yet maintains its relevance for the world in which we live? There are some patterns within the Sermon that may help.

First, our interpretation must be guided by the unique awareness of God that permeates the Sermon. In the Sermon God is the Heavenly Parent whose name is to be honored (6:9). This Father is perfect and requires perfection of others (5:48). God's Law will not pass away (5:18). Consequently the demands of the Sermon must be taken with all seriousness as expressions of God's will.

Second, the program for implementation of God's will is the Kingdom of God. This Kingdom is not so much a place as it is a condition: the Kingdom of God is wherever and whenever God is reigning. The Kingdom of God stands at the center of Jesus' preaching. The Kingdom has future dimensions (13:36-43, 47-50), but the key focus falls on the present (4:17; 13:31-33, 44, 45). This Kingdom is near at hand and is available to those who answer the invitation of Jesus. The demands and the possibilities presented in the Sermon must be understood within this framework. They are not new rules or general principals of conduct; they are components of the Kingdom of God.

The priority of God and the nearness of the Kingdom undergird a third guide for interpretation: the radical demands of the Sermon are based upon the extraordinary grace of God. Because they have experienced God's forgiveness, believers must forgive all who wrong them—friend and foe alike. Because the believers have experienced God's mercy, they are to be merciful. Disciples are to be perfect and complete because of who God is and how God has acted toward them. Believers can ask and seek and knock because they know a gracious Parent stands at the door. Consequently there is to be a direct correlation between God's treatment of us and our treatment of others. The grace of God is the experience and motivation that undergirds all Christian discipleship. These demands and the discipline they require are equally an expression of God's grace in the life of the disciple. This insistent grace provides the key to understanding the ethical demands of the Sermon.

Finally, the demands of life in the Kingdom are related to our present situation. They cannot be reserved for another people or another place or another time. The Sermon demands that we pray "Your kingdom come, your will be done, on earth as in heaven" (6:10). The nearness of the Kingdom can be seen in the birds of the air that fly over our head and in the flowers of the field that grow beneath our feet. The time of the Kingdom is now; the place of the Kingdom is here.

These principles of interpretation, gleaned from the Sermon itself, may help us to experience the reality of the Sermon as our own reality. Salt only works when it is applied to something, and it only works when it remains salty. In a similar way we must take the Sermon seriously without removing it from the stage of everyday life. Here the vision of the Anabaptists is relevant:

We shall not believe, they said, that the Sermon on the Mount or any other vision that He had is only a heavenly vision meant but to keep His followers in tension until the last great day, but we shall practice what He taught, believing that where He walked we can by his grace follow in his steps.[7]

Thus, our study of the Sermon must maintain both its seriousness and its relevance. We will be helped to do this by remembering that behind the words of the Sermon stands the divine presence and divine imperative of God. God's will is to be sovereign over all of life, and this will is expressed in the program of the Kingdom of God. Behind the overwhelming demands of the Kingdom lifestyle lies our experience of God's extraordinary grace. God intends that this Kingdom become a reality in our own lives and in our own world. With these principles in mind, we turn to the Sermon on the Mount.

The Beginning
(5:1-2)

Matthew places the Sermon on the Mount in the midst of his story of Jesus' ministry. Following the story of Jesus' origins (1:1–2:23), Matthew tells of the beginning of Jesus' ministry. Jesus' story begins with the work of John the Baptist, who baptizes Jesus (3:1-17). Jesus undergoes a time of testing (4:1-11), then he is proclaimed as God's light for both Jews and Gentiles (4:12-16). Matthew 4:17 is programmatic for Matthew's story of Jesus: "From that time Jesus began to proclaim, 'Repent, for the Kingdom of Heaven stands near.'" Jesus gathers first the disciples (4:18-22) and then the crowds (4:23-25). Matthew then presents his central evidence of Jesus' call to the Kingdom—the Sermon on the Mount (5:1–7:29).

Matthew is an organizer, and the Sermon reflects his patterns of careful arrangement. As usual, Matthew provides a clear introduction and conclusion to the material he presents. Matthew 5:1-2 sets the stage for the Sermon by telling of the place, the people, and the purpose.

The place is a mountainside, which calls to mind the many Old Testament stories in which God works upon the mountain for the people of Israel. The Jewish reader would especially recall the stories in which Moses brought the Law down from Mount Sinai.

Two descriptions of the people are given: crowds and disciples. When Jesus sees the crowds, he goes up to teach. He calls to him a special group who are labeled as disciples, or "learners." Jesus has chosen a special place and called aside certain people.

The purpose of this is soon clear: he begins to teach them. In this way Matthew helps us to see Jesus as the Teacher whom God has sent to instruct and lead the people. While others may find the key to God's will in texts or traditions, Matthew insists that Jesus' proclamation of the Kingdom provides the key to righteousness.

The stage is set. The audience is in place. The Teacher is about to begin. Those who wish to learn should listen well.

Outline

I. The Beginning (5:1-2)
   A. The Place (5:1)
   B. The People (5:1)
   C. The Purpose (5:2)
II. The Kingdom Lifestyle (5:3-16)
   A. The Beatitudes: The Nature and Consequence of the Kingdom Lifestyle (5:3-12)
      1. First blessing: the poor in spirit (5:3)
      2. Second blessing: those who mourn (5:4)
      3. Third blessing: the meek (5:5)
      4. Fourth blessing: hungering, thirsting for righteousness (5:6)
      5. Fifth blessing: the merciful (5:7)
      6. Sixth blessing: the pure in heart (5:8)
      7. Seventh blessing: the peacemakers (5:9)
      8. Eighth blessing: the persecuted (5:10-12)
   B. The Expression of the Kingdom Lifestyle (5:13-16)
      1. The image of salt (5:13)
      2. The image of light (5:14-16)

III. The Kingdom Lifestyle and Law (5:17-48)
    A. The Nature of Law (5:17-20)
        1. Jesus and the Law (5:17-18)
        2. Disciples and the Law (5:19-20)
    B. Examples of Law (5:21-48)
        1. Murder (5:21-26)
        2. Adultery (5:27-30)
        3. Divorce (5:31-32)
        4. Oaths (5:33-37)
        5. Revenge (5:38-42)
        6. Love (5:43-48)
IV. The Kingdom Lifestyle and Worship (6:1-34)
    A. The Nature of Worship (6:1)
    B. Examples of Worship (6:2-34)
        1. Giving (6:2-4)
        2. Prayer (6:5-15)
        3. Fasting (6:16-18)
        4. The Danger of idolatry (6:19-34)
V. The Kingdom Lifestyle and Others (7:1-6)
    A. Judging Others (7:1-5)
        1. The principle (7:1-2)
        2. The lesson of the log and the speck (7:3-5)
    B. Discretion: The Lesson of the Dogs and the Pigs (7:6)
VI. The Kingdom Lifestyle and Self (7:7-27)
    A. The Principle of Availability (7:7-14)
        1. God is available to us (7:7-12)
        2. Becoming available to God: the gate and the road (7:13-14)
    B. The Principle of Consistency (7:15-23)
        1. A tree and its fruit (7:15-20)
        2. Words and lifestyle (7:21)
        3. Deeds and relationships (7:22-23)
    C. The Picture of life (7:24-27)
        1. Hearing and doing: the wise person (7:24-25)
        2. Hearing and not doing: the foolish person (7:26-27)
VII. Conclusion (7:28-29)

Discussion Questions

Engaging the Text

1. Matthew and Luke present different forms of the Sermon. What are some explanations for this variation? What does this say about their purposes for this material? About the inspiration of these passages?
2. Why has the Sermon had such a wide impact throughout history? Does this impact have to do primarily with its language? Its message? Its source? Which of the people influenced by the Sermon do you find most interesting?
3. What do you think is the most important danger to avoid when reading the Sermon? What is the most important guide for understanding the Sermon?

For Further Reflection

1. How would you respond to the following statement? "I will become a Christian when I see Christians practice the Sermon on the Mount."
2. To what degree is the Sermon a matter for personal faith? To what degree does the Sermon address social and political questions?
3. Is there an urgent personal question you should reevaluate in light of the Sermon on the Mount? Are there specific social and political issues in this week's news that might be addressed by the Sermon? In what way?
4. What role might the Sermon on the Mount play in Christian teaching? In preaching and worship? In evangelism?

Notes

¹Cited in Pinchas Lapide, *The Sermon on the Mount: Utopia or Program for Action?* trans. A. Swidler (Maryknoll NY: Orbis Books, 1986 [1982]) 3.

²Ibid., 44.

³Paul provides a clear example of this process. He was himself a Pharisee, and prior to his conversion he traveled to various towns seeking to enforce his view of faith. After his call to preach the risen Christ, Paul traveled widely through the Graeco-Roman world. He typically began his work in the local synagogue, seeking to convince Jewish worshipers that the key to God's work lay not in the Law, but in the risen Christ. Only after his rejection in various synagogues do we find Paul preaching in the marketplaces and worshiping in house churches.

⁴For a helpful summary of the impact of the Sermon, see W. Kissinger, *The Sermon on the Mount: A History of Interpretation and Bibliography*, ATLA Bibliography Series, no. 3 (Metuchen NJ: Scarecrow Press, 1975).

⁵*The Preaching of Augustine: "Our Lord's Sermon on the Mount,"* ed. Jeroslav Pelikan (Philadelphia: Fortress Press, 1973) I.1.1.

⁶The Anabaptist heritage continues today among a few Anabaptist churches and among groups such as the Mennonites, the Amish, and the Hutterites.

⁷Harold Bender, "The Anabaptist Vision," *The Recovery of the Anabaptist Vision*, ed G. Hershberger (Scottdale PA: Herald Press, 1957) 54.

The Kingdom Lifestyle

(Matt 5:3-16)

The Sermon on the Mount presents the lifestyle that belongs to those who would follow Jesus. Matthew makes it clear that the call to discipleship precedes the demands of the Sermon. Following his baptism (3:13-17) and his temptation (4:1-16), Jesus begins a ministry of preaching. His message is this: "Repent, for the kingdom of heaven stands near" (v. 17). At that point Jesus calls his first disciples (vv. 18-22). With these disciples he goes throughout Galilee preaching the gospel of the Kingdom and also teaching and healing (v. 23). As a result, crowds from many places follow Jesus (vv. 24-25).

Thus, Matthew presents the teachings in chapters 5–7 as instructions in discipleship. The description and the demands of the Kingdom are given to those who have already come under the claim of the Kingdom. Consequently the Beatitudes and the material that follows should not be understood as requirements to be met or accomplishments to be achieved in order to find God's acceptance; they represent instead the demands God places upon those who have entered into the way of the Kingdom. Eduard Schweizer concludes, "That the Sermon on the Mount from Matthew, as well as the Sermon on the Plain from Luke, begins with the Blessings reveals the awareness that only God's gracious encouragement . . . can stand at the beginning."[1]

Matthew prefers to speak of the Kingdom of Heaven rather than the Kingdom of God. This reflects Matthew's sensitivity to his Jewish listeners. Because of the second commandment (Exod 20:7), Jewish people were hesitant to use the name of God lest they mispronounce or misuse it. They often used circumlocutions or abbreviations to avoid direct use of God's name. This practice is likely behind Matthew's preference to speak of the Kingdom of Heaven. In reality there is no difference between the Kingdom of Heaven and the Kingdom of God. The demands for disciples begin with a portrait of the Kingdom lifestyle.

Nature and Consequence
(5:3-12)

The opening discussion on the Kingdom lifestyle employs a pattern familiar to Jewish listeners—the blessing or beatitude. Arriving pilgrims are blessed in the psalms of the Old Testament (Ps 84:5,12; 128:1). A series of blessings is pronounced on those who practice wisdom in Sirach 25:7-11. Thus, this type of blessing belonged to the Jewish heritage behind the Sermon. Matthew and Luke make quite different use of the blessing formula.[2]

Matthew employs eight blessings that share a similar form. The eighth (5:11) is followed by an expansion of the persecution theme, which employs a different form (vv. 11-12). Some commentaries will count verses 11 and 12 as a ninth beatitude. For Matthew, the Beatitudes describe the nature of life in the Kingdom and the consequences of that lifestyle. These blessings should not be understood as entrance requirements or as steps to be achieved on the way to acceptance by God. They represent God's demands upon those already accepted into the Kingdom. The Blessings should not be seen as universals or as laws of nature. For example, the fifth blessing promises mercy for the merciful, but the eighth blessing recognizes that the merciful are sometimes met with violence and abuse. These blessings are not legal or natural equations, but deal with a new set of correlations at work in the Kingdom. They point to a personal transformation that must be lived out in the context of community. They describe a new law of return, set in place by the Kingdom, in which the weak are not to be crushed by the strong. They represent the hope of a new way of life inaugurated in the reality of the Kingdom.

While these blessings do not immediately change all violent leaders into meek and righteous people, they do change the life of the believer. Violence and power and greed can no longer set the agenda or control the life of believers, for they have entered into the reign of God. A new environment or existence is becoming reality in the lives of those who enter the Kingdom. These Kingdom values are to become the defining mark of the church, the Christian community. This transformation may also affect society. By practicing the lifestyle of the Kingdom, individual believers and Christian communities may help to create this new reality in the world about them. This new environment, these new codes of existence, can only be inaugurated by those who share in the Kingdom of God.

The first four blessings point to states of existence: poor in spirit, mourning, meek, desiring righteousness. These are characteristics we would not usually associate with winners! Few people would see these traits as the keys to success in business or politics or sports. It should come as something of a surprise that Jesus would pronounce such people as blessed. Surely Jesus does not mean that poverty is good or that grief makes one happy. Becoming poor does not make one a Christian, and mourning does not always lead to comfort. What, then, is the connection to these states of existence?

Matthew points out the unusual correspondence between these conditions and the reality of the Kingdom. First, there is a surprise here: even the poor in spirit, the sad, the meek, and those starving for goodness may enjoy the blessings of God. Indeed, it is these people who are most open and most receptive to the help of God. This blessing says more about God and God's Kingdom than about the quality of their lives. God's reign is such that even the little people—indeed, especially the little people—have a share in God's blessings. How blessed are those whose hands are empty and whose hearts are open, for they may be filled by the Kingdom of God!

The last four of the blessings point to patterns of conduct: showing mercy, being pure in heart, making peace, being persecuted. Those who carry out such conduct were not expected to succeed in the violent world in which Jesus lived. If we are honest, this conduct is not typical of leaders in our time either. Again, there is a surprising correspondence between this type of conduct and the Kingdom: even the merciful, the pure, the peaceful, and the oppressed may succeed by God's standards. Indeed, it is only these who will succeed with God!

People who seek to live moral lives may exhibit a number of these traits. Non-Christians may be meek, and many seek justice for nonreligious reasons. Thus, the individual traits listed here are not exclusively Christian values. Nonetheless the linkage of these eight traits into a single package points to Christian faith rather than to isolated moral ideals. Taken as a whole, these values point to life that has been transformed by the call of Jesus into the Kingdom of God.

The first four blessings focus upon proper attitudes; the last four point to proper deeds. This combination of attitude and action echoes the larger demands of the Sermon. Thus, the Blessings present a code of discipleship reflecting the wholistic lifestyle (attitudes and actions) that characterizes life under God's rule.

The seventh blessing exemplifies this quality. While peace is often mentioned as a desired moral value, some clarification is needed. Many who speak of peace have in mind the concept of "keeping the peace." Often this means nothing more than preserving the *status quo*. For example, the era of *Pax Romana* (Roman Peace) in which Christianity arose was characterized by brutal military oppression. There was quiet and stability because Rome suppressed all its challengers! Others see peace as a value to be imposed. Military troops are often sent into troubled areas as "peacekeeping forces." During the Cold War of the 1980s one nuclear missile was nicknamed "the peacekeeper." Peace that is imposed by force or peace that accepts an unjust stability stands far from the values of Jesus.

The seventh beatitude blesses those who *make* peace. This blessing assumes a situation of violence and injustice that is transformed by the creative intervention of peacemakers. The tools for the construction of such a peace are mercy, mourning, meekness, poverty, purity, and justice. Thus, the peace of the seventh beatitude is no abstract moral platitude; it is a costly peace won through the sweat and sacrifice of discipleship. Both attitude and action are involved. The task of peacemaking assumes a personal experience of transformation and a singular commitment to discipleship. The task of peacemaking requires energy and endurance that can be sustained only by God's presence in the life of the disciple. Peacemaking begins with God's gracious initiative toward the individual. One who has been transformed by experiencing peace with God will, of nature and necessity, practice peacemaking. This is the blessing that awaits those who practice peace: they will be called children of God. Thus, peacemaking, as with the Blessings in their entirety, is a sign of discipleship that marks the life of those who have embraced Jesus' call to the Kingdom.

It is noteworthy in the Beatitudes that the promised rewards cohere with the activity of those blessed. Those seeking righteousness will find it; those demonstrating mercy will receive mercy. These blessings do not present a formula for power or wealth such as "you will be recognized for your humility" or "do the right thing, and you will go far." We would do violence to the Sermon to interpret these formulas as keys to happiness or success by any worldly standard. Those who live and act as the Beatitudes describe will open themselves to the rewards of the Kingdom: comfort, righteousness, mercy, right relation to God, and persecution. Those who practice this lifestyle should not expect to own the bank and to rule the world, but they should expect to live under God's gracious reign. That is reward enough.

Thus, the Beatitudes do not provide required steps to be achieved before entering God's rule. They do not provide universals or laws of natural return in which good always conquers evil. Neither do they call us to be naive. These blessings point instead to attitudes and actions that are congruent with life under God's reign. This is the new reality to be experienced in the life of the transformed Christian and in the transformed community.

We would do wrong to hear this message as innocent and unoffensive. In a world controlled by the strong and the wealthy and the powerful, it must have come as a shock to Jesus' hearers to realize the correspondence between the life of the meek and the blessings of the Kingdom. This message would come as a threat to those content with their power, luxury, or righteousness. But for those who needed God's help the most, this realization must have come as a comfort. At the heart of the gospel is the good news that the poor and empty and oppressed stand near to God; or rather, God stands near to them.

In the realm of the Kingdom the poor and the mourning can be blessed; the meek shall endure; righteousness and mercy may be found; purity of heart means something; peacemaking is divinely sanctioned; and the persecuted have a home. Here is a radically new agenda for life; here is a new law of return; here is the beginning of a new reality. Individuals and communities that claim to follow Jesus must live out these values. Blessed are those who already participate.

Expression
(5:13-16)

The Kingdom is more than a series of blessings to be experienced; it is a way of life to be practiced. Matthew 5:13-16 uses two images to talk about ways in which we can express the values of the Kingdom in daily life.

First, believers are called "the salt of the earth" (v. 13). This is not so much a goal to be obtained, but a description of who we already are. Here the salt is encouraged to live up to its reputation—to be salty! Thus, the real focus falls on how Christians are to express the new life they already share in the Kingdom.

Jesus' use of such word pictures invites us to think about different aspects of these symbols for the Kingdom. Salt works in several ways: it heals, preserves, and flavors. These traits can become further images for discipleship. The warning about becoming unsalty is also informative. From a scientific standpoint salt really never loses its saltiness. However, salt can become so diluted with something else that it is no longer effective. This reality highlights a quandry we face every day. Salt is no good unless you apply it to something or mix it with something (such as food!); in doing so, we face the danger of losing the effect of the salt. There is a further image here: salt, if overdone, can be painful or offensive.

All of these aspects of Jesus' image invite us to think about our own discipleship. Saltiness is not a goal for the believer but a given: "You are the salt of the earth." Disciples cannot reserve their piety for sacred centers or personal experience; Christians are to be mixed in and applied to the world, for "you are the salt *of the earth*." Yet, by mixing with the world, there is the danger of becoming so diluted by the world that we are no longer effective. But we cannot escape this quandry. Jesus invites us to take these risks and to live out the realities of the Kingdom in our own world.

A similar image is found in verses 14-16: "You are the light of the world." Again, there is no thought here of how to become light, for that has already happened. The real concern is how Christians can put into effect the light they share! Light hidden or reserved is useless and foolish. When light is properly focused and directed it can light up a house or a way or even the world. Disciples are to provide a light for other humans to find their way to God. Elsewhere the Sermon admonishes Christians not to practice piety to be seen by others, but here others are to see their good works. We should think not of a spotlight drawing attention to an actor on a stage, but to a streetlight brightening up a dangerous path.

Again, there is risk when one engages the world with Christian faith: you may overdo it, and you may get lost among the crowds. Disciples are commanded to take that risk. If properly done, this stand will bring glory to God (v. 16). This witness provides key expression and evidence of the Kingdom lifestyle. One who has experienced the blessings of God's reign must shine forth as a light that draws others to the Heavenly Parent. This is the task given to individuals and communities who claim to live under God's rule.

It is this engagement with the world as salt and light that offers the most difficult—and the most productive—challenge for the church. The great reformer Martin Luther, realizing that he could not follow God's call in isolation, returned from the monastery to live in the world. Dietrich Bonhoeffer, the German pastor and professor, initially fled to the United States to escape Hitler's reign, but soon returned to Germany, saying:

> I have come to the conclusion that I have made a mistake in coming to America. I must live through this difficult period of our national history with the Christian people of Germany.[3]

This engagement often produces discomfort for the world and difficulties for the church. Such tension is both healthy and necessary. Clarence Jordan held this view:

> Whenever tension ceases to exist between the church and the world, one of two things has happened: Either the world has been completely converted to Christ and his Way, or the church has watered down and compromised its original heritage. In the latter position, the church, due to its weakness, loses its influence and is discarded.[4]

It is precisely in this engagement with the world that the church tests its worth. Clarence Jordan further declared:

> That church is yet to be found which long survived in the midst of race prejudice, national pride, militarism, and exploitation without lifting up a mighty "Thus saith the Lord." To be sure, when it so speaks, it becomes a persecuted church, but it is always so virile that men find extreme difficulty in ignoring it or trampling it under foot.[5]

Thus, the church is called to be God's chosen agent of change at work in the world. To enter into the arena of the world is to risk losing the distinct purity of Christian faith. Failure to engage the world with the gospel is to ensure losing both the gospel and the world. Conflict, and perhaps persecution, await the Christian and the Christian community who engage the world with the teachings of Jesus. But Christians, as God's salt and light, can exist with authentic worth nowhere else.

Joel Chandler Harris collected a series of African-American stories in which a sly fox is forever chasing Brer Rabbit.[6] One day the fox succeeds in catching the rabbit, but he cannot decide what to do with him. "I think I'll barbeque you," says Brer Fox. "Roast me if you wish," says Brer Rabbit. "Just don't throw me into the briar patch." "It's so much trouble to kindle a fire," says Brer Fox, "that I think I'll hang you." "Hang me as high as you please," says Brer Rabbit, "but please don't throw me into that briar patch." "I have no string," says the fox, "so I guess I'll have to drown you." "Drown me as deep as you please," says Brer Rabbit, "but don't throw me into that briar patch." "There's no water here," says Brer Fox, "so I guess I'll have to skin you." "Skin me, Brer Fox," says Brer Rabbit. "Snatch out my eyeballs, tear out my ears by the roots, and cut off my legs," he says, "but do please, Brer Fox, don't throw me into that briar patch." Since Brer Fox wants to hurt Brer Rabbit as much as possible, he does just that. What the outwitted fox does not know, of course, is that the briar patch is really the home of Brer Rabbit. "Bred and born in the briar patch," says Brer Rabbit. "Bred and born in the briar patch."

The Sermon on the Mount calls for a discipleship that encounters and engages the cultures in which we live. As Christians, the world is precisely the place where we are destined to live out our discipleship; the world is our briar patch.

Conclusion

Surprisingly, this opening discussion on the Kingdom lifestyle is not imperative or even suggestive: it does not tell Christians what we are to become. It is, instead, constitutive: it urges us to live out the fullness of what we already are as God's children—salt and light.

While these lines encourage believers and Christian communities to live out the fullness of their discipleship, non-Christians are not excluded from this portrait. Addressed to disciples, the Sermon also speaks to the crowds. To those on the outside the Sermon provides an offer—an earthy, salty, illuminating invitation—to share in God's gracious rule.

Discussion Questions

Engaging the Text

1. Why is it important that the call to the Kingdom precedes the demands of the Sermon?
2. Why do you think Jesus used a customary form for the Blessings?
3. What do you think Jesus' audience found surprising or shocking in his blessings? What do you find surprising or shocking?
4. Why do you think Jesus chose images from everyday life to speak about God's work? How would this language affect his audience, especially if they were accustomed to "religious" language? How does this language affect you as a listener?

For Further Reflection

1. In what ways do we tend to dilute or obscure the impact of the Beatitudes?
2. How would you paraphrase the Blessings, using specific situations from your own world?
3. How do the images of salt and light relate to your devotional life? To your social life? To political concerns?
4. What are some other images from everyday life that can focus the demands for life in the Kingdom?
5. If the Beatitudes assume that one has experienced God's mercy, how could you use them to speak to a non-Christian?

Notes

¹Eduard Schweizer, *Die Bergpredigt* (Gottingen: Vandenhoeck & Ruprecht, 1982) 8.

²Matthew has eight blessings with an addition to the last one; Luke has four blessings followed by four Woes. Matthew emphasizes present realities; Luke emphasizes future rewards or loss. A comparison of Matthew 5:3-12 and Luke 6.20-26 also reveals how Matthew and Luke give quite different forms of the blessings they have in common.

³Dietrich Bonhoeffer, *The Cost of Discipleship* (New York: MacMillan, 1963) 25.

⁴Clarence Jordan, *Sermon on the Mount*, rev. ed. (Valley Forge PA: Judson Press, 1974) 41.

⁵Ibid., 41-42.

⁶Joel Chandler Harris, *The Complete Tales of Uncle Remus* (Boston: Houghton & Mifflin, 1955).

The Kingdom Lifestyle and Law

(Matt 5:17-48)

When one begins a new course of study, attempts a new sport, or enters a new country, a process of reorientation is required. When beginning such adventures one must first learn the rules. A person who enters the Kingdom of God will experience a similar situation. What are the standards for living under God's reign? This question would be of particular interest to Matthew's Jewish audience. Their lives had been guided by the Torah, the Jewish Law. From their birth to their death and at all stages between the Law of Moses provided a constant guide. For those who have entered into the Kingdom, the role of the Law becomes a crucial issue. Have Christians abandoned the Law? Does Jesus replace the Law with a new set of rules? The relationship of the Kingdom lifestyle and the Law is addressed in Matthew 5:17-48.

Nature of the Law
(5:17-20)

Since Jesus was a faithful Jew and all of his earliest followers came from Jewish faith, it was necessary for the Christian movement to clarify its relationship with Judaism. At the center of this ongoing discussion was the role of the Law of Moses for Jesus and his followers. This question would be of particular importance for Matthew's community. The Sermon clarifies the role of Law for those who have entered the Kingdom. Once again, the context of these teachings is important. Even as the Ten Commandments and the Law of Moses were given as a part of God's covenant with Israel, so the laws sketched out in the Sermon belong to the context of the call to the Kingdom. Attention is first given to some basic principles (vv. 17-20) and then to specific examples (vv. 21-48).

Jesus and the Law
(5:17-18)

Paul and other early Christians were often accused of being lawless people who wished to destroy what Moses had taught. This accusation was leveled against Jesus. Jesus first clarifies his own relation to God's Law. He has not come to destroy this Law, but to fulfill it (v. 17). Verse 18 reinforces his claim in several ways. First, Jesus employs a formula that emphasizes the truth of his claim: "Amen, I say to you . . ." Then Jesus emphasizes the durability of the Law: it will outlast the heavens and the earth. Finally, Jesus highlights the reliability of the Law: not one little part will fail.[1] This explanation represents Jesus' view of God's Law.

We will discover soon that Jesus understands God's Law in quite a different way than others. For Jesus, the Law is more than just the traditions of Israel or even the written codes of the Old Testament. In the Sermon Jesus will show that the Law has more to do with God's intentions for humanity than with any specific set of codes or rules. For the moment, however, Jesus confirms the irreplaceable and irreducible role of the Law.

Disciples and the Law
(5:19-20)

The attitude of Jesus must be shared by those who live in the Kingdom. The practice and the teaching of Jesus' followers must confirm God's Law, not reduce it. The opponent of the Law will be least under God's reign. In contrast, one who practices and teaches the Law will be great in the Kingdom. Thus, Jesus calls those who have entered the Kingdom not to abandon the Law, but to fulfill it in what they do and in what they teach. Matthew is eager for his community and his opponents to understand that Christian faith fulfills, not abandons, the Law of God.

This discussion on the principles of Law ends in a shocking climax. Here Jesus points to the degree of obedience demanded of his followers. Those listening to Jesus would have been shocked at what he demanded, for he insisted that common people practice a righteousness greater than that of their religious leaders! Indeed, no one could enter the Kingdom unless their righteousness exceed that of the scribes and Pharisees! While we often think of Pharisees and their scribes as insincere and hypocritical, they were in fact dedicated beyond imagination to keeping God's Law. Certainly it would be impossible to be more zealous or give more attention to detail than did these religious leaders. It is shocking then when Jesus demands that his follows be more righteous than their leaders.

What can this command mean? Certainly Jesus must have a different perspective and expectation of what it means to obey the Law. This viewpoint will become evident shortly. For the moment, however, the nature of Law in the life of the Kingdom has been clarified. Jesus has come to complete, not empty, the Law, and he demands that his followers teach and practice a higher righteousness. Followers of Jesus are to be more, not less, obedient than the followers of Moses. Matthew emphasizes this claim in view of the situation his own community faces. It is the Christian community under the instruction of Jesus that lives out the full intent of the Law. The extravagant grace they have experienced under God's reign is to be accompanied by extraordinary discipline.

Many churches today err by demanding discipline with little attention to grace; others err by offering grace with no demand for discipline. The call of Jesus insists the experience of grace must be expressed in discipleship. Some examples of this obedience follow.

Examples of Law
(5:21-48)

Having stated the principles of how Kingdom and Law relate, the Sermon gives practical illustrations of how those under God's reign are to practice obedience. Six examples are presented: murder, adultery, divorce, oaths, revenge, and love.

Murder
(5:21-26)

Jesus insists that the ethics of those in the Kingdom surpass the conduct previously required under the Law. It might surprise some persons to learn that much of what Jesus cites as the old tradition is not simply the oral tradition of the Jewish religious leaders; at times Jesus cites the Old Testament and requires that his followers go further. In Matthew 5:21 Jesus cites one of the Ten Commandments: "Do not commit murder" (Exod 20:13) and notes the threat of judgment for those who do. He then uses a stark formula of contrast ("But I say to you . . .") to set his own teaching over against the former traditions. Jesus does not soften the Old Testament requirement not to murder; indeed, he makes it stricter. Jesus insists that one who is angry with another person is also liable to judgment (Matt 5:22). While the old standard commanded us not to murder, the new command of Jesus forbids us to treat another person with anger or contempt (as exemplified in language such as "fool" or "moron").

While the old tradition focused on the act that kills another, Jesus' command focuses on the larger attitudes and relationships that precede such actions. Two practical examples demonstrate Jesus' command to be rightly related to other people. First, worship of God is improper and insincere while one is at odds with another human. Worship should be postponed until proper relationships are restored (v. 24). The second image demonstrates the potential danger of broken and unjust relationships. Jesus uses an example of the debtor's court of his own day. An unsettled dispute may lead to court, and court may lead to prison. Better to settle such issues now than to let them grow!

The result of these images is a radical demand upon the followers of Jesus. Behind the strict legal command not to murder lies the issue of attitude and relationship. The Law can forbid and punish murder, but it cannot prevent it. In contrast, Jesus' command to be quickly reconciled with others prevents the anger and division that lead to violence and murder. Jesus deals with the cause of the disease and not just its symptoms! While the old command simply forbids the worst outcome of anger and violence, Jesus' command takes the initiative toward a reconciliation that limits anger and violence. In this way the command of Jesus exceeds the specifics of law. His command also exceeds the limited power of law. Ancient and modern legal codes limited murder by imposing strict penalties. They could not, however, prevent the desire to murder. Many folks would murder if they could get away with it! The command of Jesus addresses both the consequence and the cause; it demands that we become righteous people who practice reconciliation rather than violence.

Typical interpretations of the sixth commandment ("You shall not murder") deal with exceptions to this rule: self-defense, law enforcement, military service, and capital punishment. Jesus deals with none of these. Instead of offering exceptions to the sixth commandment, Jesus points to the underlying principles of human behavior and to the real intent of God's Law. Throughout its history the church has shown more concern for exceptions and negations of this command than for its underlying intent.

The strongest interpretation of Jesus' teaching on murder is found among the Anabaptists and their descendants. In their earliest confession of faith, the Schleitheim Articles of 1527, this is one of only seven issues addressed. Christians are forbidden to bear arms, even "against the wicked for the protection and defense of the good, or for the sake of love."[2] Christians are further forbidden to pass sentence in worldly disputes and are not to serve as magistrates because of their prior commitment to serve Christ peaceably. "The worldly are armed with steel and iron, but Christians are armed with the armor of God, with truth, righteousness, peace, faith, salvation, and with the Word of God."[3]

While Christians have sometimes died by the sword at the hands of others, the church has too frequently offered its blessings to those who wielded the sword. Indeed, the church itself has often wielded the sword and sanctioned murder in the name of God. This is no easy matter for Christians ancient or modern, but the command of Jesus stands. Jesus forbids not only the worst consequences of violence and hatred, but also their very causes. This is the higher righteousness that Jesus demands.

There is another key aspect to Jesus' command: one cannot be right with God until one is right with others. Thus, there is a strong correlation between participation in the Kingdom and reconciliation with others. Those who have not killed may not be righteous; they may just be cowards. Jesus demands more. If one is to be rightly related to God, then one must practice right relationships with other humans (v. 24). This is the greater righteousness of the Kingdom.

Thus, Jesus is not content to argue over trivial aspects and exceptions to God's Law. He is concerned instead for the spirit and intent that underlie these commands. Jesus is concerned that our codes of behavior express and fulfill God's will.

Adultery
(5:27-30)

Jesus takes a similar approach to the question of adultery. While the Ten Commandments may forbid and punish adultery (Exod 20:14), they do not prevent the impulse. Thus, we cannot equate keeping the rules with being righteous. Many would practice adultery if they were assured of not being caught! The command of Jesus moves beyond the letter of the Law to embrace the attitude behind true obedience. Jesus defines an adultery that is measured in attitude rather than in act alone. The seriousness of the adulterous attitude is emphasized through dramatic images such as plucking out the eye or cutting off the hand. Just as a surgeon removes a cancerous member in order to save a person's life, so the disciple is threatened by attitudes that are adulterous. Jesus again moves beyond the keeping of the rules to the underlying issues that motivate human action. His new command forbids not only the illicit sexual act, but also the very desires that lead to the act. This is the greater righteousness that Jesus demands.

Divorce
(5:31-32)

The next contrast between the old tradition and the command of Jesus deals with the issue of divorce. The old tradition insisted upon a certificate of divorce when a man left a woman (the idea of a woman divorcing a man in Old Testament times was hardly thinkable). In reality the certificate of divorce was a compassionate requirement. Prior to the command of Moses a Jewish male could probably divorce his wife by verbal decree. This oral divorce meant that the woman would be thrown out with no legal documentation. In the streets or in the marketplace she lacked proof that she was no longer bound to her husband, and she could easily be seen as an adulteress or a prostitute. The legal certificate gave the woman proof that her husband had sent her away. Thus, the written divorce represented a judicious attempt to make the best of a bad situation.

Jesus demands more. Since Judaism gave the power of divorce to the man, Jesus' command focuses on the male perspective. Husbands are forbidden to divorce their wives except on the ground of unfaithfulness. To do so is to make the wife an adulteress, for her marriage vows have been broken. Though the husband initiates the divorce, the wife suffers the broken marriage. This is further complicated if she must marry again in order to survive (the idea of a self-supporting single woman would be rare in this time period). Thus, the divorce imposed by a man upon his wife places her unwillingly in a role tainted by the suspicion of adultery.

Jesus pursues the other side of this issue, still from the male perspective. If a man marries a woman who has been sent away by her husband, then he also commits adultery. The perception that he is married to another man's wife will linger over the second marriage. If the desire of the second husband for the wife played any role in the divorce, then this perception is realized. In either case the question of adultery clings to the second marriage.

All of these requirements must be examined against the social context of the Old Testament, then against the Jewish and Roman legal codes of Jesus' own day. These commands cannot be reduced to a simple legal requirement applicable to any time or situation. Nor can we expect the governments of pluralistic societies to enforce Christian values. Nonetheless it is important that we not miss the radical nature of Jesus' teaching on this issue.

First, Jesus takes divorce seriously. Meeting the legal requirements for separation and divorce is not the end of the matter for Jesus. The real focus of the issue is marital faithfulness and endurance. Building upon the instruction concerning adultery, these sayings point to the inner attitudes that precede the breakdown of marriage.

Secondly, Jesus takes the side of the weaker partner. It is the woman who suffered most from divorce in the time of Jesus, and he gives greater attention to her suffering. His commands highlight the pain and injustice the divorced woman suffered, and he takes steps to address that pain and injustice.

Before we ask about the relevance of Jesus' teaching on divorce for our own time, we must see it in its own context. Over against a legalistic, male-oriented view that served the needs of the abuser, Jesus sets forth a greater righteousness based on faithfulness and endurance.

We cannot expect the legal code of a nation to create such Christian values. Legal codes can forbid adultery, and harsh governments might prevent the act of adultery, but they cannot create good marriages. Here is a gift and witness the church can offer within a pluralistic society. The ideals of strong, faithful, compassionate marriages fulfill the will of God and offer a key witness to the faith of the church. While the church cannot expect governments to enforce Christian views of morality, the church can articulate and model the will of God to the larger society.

Oaths
(5:33-37)

The old standard required that oaths made to God be kept without exception. Beyond this standard there developed various levels of casuistry to release a person from lesser promises. As a result, the validity of the promise came to depend upon the object invoked in the oath rather than upon the integrity of the one making the promise. Jesus demands more. In his new standard the truth does not require confirmation through elaborate oaths: "Do not make an oath at all," Jesus commands. To swear by heaven or earth or even by Jerusalem is to swear indirectly by God, since these all belong to God (v. 35). Thus, these oaths are no less binding than oaths sworn to the Lord God. Oaths sworn by the head of a person carry no real meaning or power (v. 36). Thus, the whole system of greater and lesser vows collapses upon itself.

Jesus offers a simpler, more straightforward approach for disciples: yes should always mean yes; no should always mean no. Devices that obscure the truth through misdirection, diversion, or technicality are evil (v. 37), and attempts to support the truth are useless. Jesus demands that the word of a disciple stand consistently on its own as clear-eyed truth. Like earlier teachings, this saying also points to the inner attitude of the disciples: for those taking part in the Kingdom, the strength of a promise is not bound to the powers invoked, but to the integrity of the speaker.

Revenge
(5:38-42)

The next example deals with the issue of revenge. The old standard of "an eye for an eye and a tooth for a tooth" is drawn from the Old Testament (Exod 21.23-25). Like the command on adultery, this Old Testament standard represents a limitation of evil. The old standard allowed one to exact vengeance of the same kind and degree as the loss. One who lost life could take life, but one who lost an eye or a tooth could not take life. Vengeance was thus limited to an equivalent payback.

Jesus demands more. With emphatic contrast ("But I say to you") Jesus puts an end to the payback scheme. A blow to the face is not to be answered in kind. Theft of one's garment does not license recompense. Conscription into temporary military service as a courier is not to be avenged. Indeed, one who suffers these impositions is to respond with shocking complicity: turn the other cheek, offer the other garment, go the second mile, give the desired gift, loan what is requested.

We should not try to turn this command into some utilitarian law of good over evil. Those who follow this code should expect to find themselves twice-beaten and naked! This is not a logical code that makes sense in the end; it is a theological program that places one in right relation to God.

What, then, is the value of such radical, illogical behavior? At least three patterns of transformation may be observed where this nonviolent response is practiced. First, the life of the disciple is changed. Whatever else happens, the follower of Jesus is transformed into a patient, nonviolent person. The more this value is practiced, the more the disciple becomes like Jesus, who refused to answer the violence of his world in kind.

Secondly, when a disciple refuses to retaliate, the cycle of violence is disrupted. Most conflicts begin as a series of small attacks and counterattacks that escalate into full-scale warfare. In the mind of the combatants each attack justifies a larger counterattack until all sense of proportion is lost. The ethic of Jesus disrupts this process of escalation. By forfeiting the right to counterattack, the disciple may remove any justification for further attack. It is difficult and awkward to fight a war without an enemy; the ethic of Jesus may disrupt conflict by removing the believer as an active participant in violence. Martin Luther King, Jr. saw the need to break this cycle of violence:

Violence brings only temporary victories; violence, by creating many more social problems than it solves, never brings permanent peace. I am convinced that if we succumb to the temptation to use violence in our struggle for freedom, unborn generations will be the recipients of a long and desolate night of bitterness, and our chief legacy to them will be a never-ending reign of chaos. A Voice, echoing through the corridors of time, says to every intemperate Peter, "Put up thy sword." History is cluttered with the wreckage of nations that failed to follow Christ's command.[4]

Finally, the refusal to retaliate may transform the opponent. Some who could not be conquered by power and violence have surrendered to the claims of Christian love. The nonretaliation that Jesus taught exposes in singular clarity the violence of the attacker and may instigate a process of transformation. This command of Jesus stands behind the words and work of Martin Luther King, Jr., who learned from Jesus the necessity of foregoing revenge: "While abhorring segregation, we shall love the segregationist. This is the only way to create the beloved community."[5]

Love
(5:43-48)

The final example of the role of law in the Kingdom sets a new standard for love. The old standard expected love for the neighbor. Certainly this was better than hating the neighbor, but love for the neighbor was often understood as the maximal requirement: one who loved the neighbor might then be free to hate the enemy.

Jesus demands more. For him, love of the neighbor was not the end of the matter, but only the beginning. Loving those like us is not an exceptional matter, Jesus says, for tax collectors and pagans do this much. Participation in the Kingdom requires that one love the enemy! In Jesus' day the enemy was not an imagined figure who had offended in some vague way. The enemy was the Roman soldier who daily oppressed the Jewish people. The enemy was the Jewish leader who betrayed the people through corruption and incompetence. How shocking that Jesus would insist his followers love such people! Once again, this command is not logical, but theological. By loving both friends and enemies, disciples prove themselves to be God's children, for they are acting as God acts! God's graciousness, exemplified in the sunshine and the rain, is extended to all people, good and evil. This same pattern of unbounded grace is required of all who would live under God's rule. Those who have experienced God's mercy and become God's children must love as the Father loves—without distinction and without limit. This is the new standard at work in the Kingdom of God.

The various commands on the Law of the Kingdom are summarized in the conclusion to this unit (v. 48). Disciples are commanded to be perfect or complete. The examples listed are not meant to cover every detail of law, but rather to demonstrate the new standard by which disciples must live. It is not enough for believers to fulfill these six commands. Disciples are to be complete; they are to fulfill all of the Law through their life in the Kingdom. Thus, no loopholes remain, and no technicalities are valid for those who have decided to follow Jesus. No code is given to cover every situation; such lists can never be comprehensive, and they are soon outdated. Instead of a fixed list of rules, Jesus gives us a new way of life. Do all of the Law, he says. Let your righteousness exceed what is expected. Do more than the rules require, he insists. The new standard of the Kingdom is this: be perfect and complete.

How can this happen? We cannot all become lawyers, memorizing every aspect of every legal code. We are not all overachievers, giving attention to every detail. How can we avoid falling into a new kind of legalism and a new level of despair?[6] The answer is given in the last half of verse 48: "Be then complete, even as your heavenly Father is complete."

Here is the responsive grace ethic that guides the Sermon on the Mount. Disciples are to fulfill the Law not because of extraordinary commitment or achievement; disciples are to fulfill the Law because of who God is and what God has done. The complete mercy and faithfulness of God that Jesus proclaimed provides the source and catalyst for our own practice of mercy and love. Out of this experience of God's mercy we are commanded to live with extraordinary consistency and compassion. We are to live as children of God who reflect the kindness of our Parent. This is the force that energizes disciples and generates a higher righteousness. This higher righteousness is demonstrated in various examples from the Law, but it is not limited to these examples. Disciples are to practice this higher righteousness in all instances and all times, thus fulfilling God's Law.

Conclusion

Many different cultures and religions have lists of rules that guide their lives. What is distinct about the portrait of the Kingdom lifestyle and Law in Matthew 5:17-48? First, this instruction stands under the unique authority of Jesus. Over against the old standard, including some passages from the Old Testament, Jesus declares "You have heard that it was said . . . but *I* say to you. . . ." Matthew shows us that Jesus has come forth in the power of God, anointed and led by the Spirit, announcing the Kingdom of God with authority. These instructions are thus rooted in a christological base—in the person and authority of Jesus, the Teacher sent from God.

Second, these instructions are set within the context of the Kingdom of God. They do not represent elements of common law applicable to any occasion; they present instead the radical, uncommon demands placed upon those who participate in the Kingdom of God. Thus, these instructions also have a theological base—they represent the lifestyle expected for those living under God's reign. Extraordinary obedience that fulfills the intention of God's Law can be commanded, for disciples have experienced the extraordinary grace of the Heavenly Parent. The complete conduct set forth in Matthew 5:17-48 can only be realized through the call of Jesus to participate in the reign of God. This is the higher righteousness that Jesus demands.

Looking back over this discussion, it becomes evident that these laws are not universal codes applicable to every situation. These rules do not cover all aspects of human behavior. They do not even cover every detail of the topics addressed. These laws are not always practical or logical.

What these principles and examples do provide is a model and a means for Christian discipleship. Rooted in the experience of God's mercy and articulated in the authoritative teaching of Jesus, these instructions point the way for faithful discipleship as a member of the Kingdom.

These new standards cannot be imposed from above by courts or constitutions. They depend instead upon changed people to live transformed lives. It is this Kingdom lifestyle—and not codes of behavior imposed from above—that offers the most effective way to transform not only persons, but also cultures, societies, and governments. It would be the highest form of arrogance and hypocrisy for Christians to ask the government to enforce a behavior or morality not fully practiced in the church. The church that does not consistently practice the demands of Jesus can hardly ask the government to enforce these demands on others. The church that lives fully under God's reign need not ask for the government's support, for the church itself will become the salt of the earth and the light of the world.

The higher righteousness that Jesus commands belongs to the way of individual discipleship within the Kingdom, but it does not stop there. Ultimately the higher righteousness to be practiced by disciples and lived out in the church offers an attractive witness and claim upon every aspect of human life.

Discussion Questions

Engaging the Text

1. Why do you think Matthew gives so much attention to the role of the Law?

2. Why do you think Jesus and his followers were accused of abandoning the Law?
3. Jesus said, "You have heard it said. . . . But *I* say to you. . . ." What does this statement imply about Jesus and his message?
4. How are the commands given here similar to other legal codes? How are they different?

For Further Reflection

1. Most legal codes recognize some forms of justifiable homicide, yet the Sermon forbids both murder and the anger that leads to murder—no exceptions. How should a Christian deal with this conflict?
2. Are there cases where divorce is the better option or the lesser of two evils? If so, how should we deal with Jesus' teaching on divorce?
3. Should a Christian today ever take an oath?
4. Can a Christian serve in the military service and be faithful to Jesus' teaching? In government positions? In politics?
5. Can governments practice nonretaliation if attacked by other nations? Can the police follow the Sermon on the Mount?
6. Who are your enemies? What does it mean to love them as Jesus commanded?

Notes

[1] Jesus uses the term for the smallest Greek letter (*iota*) and the term for a minor mark in Hebrew (*keraia*) as graphic illustrations that no small part of the Law will fail.

[2] From Article VI of the Schleitheim Articles, cited from John H. Yoder, *The Legacy of Michael Sattler* (Scottdale PA: Herald Press, 1973) 39-41.

[3] Article VI.

[4] Martin Luther King, Jr., *Strength to Love* (London: Hodder & Stoughton, 1964) 6.

[5] Ibid., 40.

[6] These are the issues that dominated much of Paul's thinking.

The Kingdom Lifestyle and Worship

(Matt 6:1-34)

For anyone entering a new religious movement, the question of proper worship is important. Where does one worship and when? What rituals and symbols are appropriate? What type of prayer is proper? How does worship shape one's lifestyle? These questions would be especially important to Matthew's community in the last part of the first century. They could no longer worship at the Temple in Jerusalem, for the Romans had destroyed in it 70 CE. Many followers of Jesus were probably excluded from the Jewish synagogues by the time Matthew wrote. If one is called to a new religious experience within the Kingdom of God, what is the proper worship that should accompany this new life? Matthew's discussion of these questions follows

The Nature of Worship
(6:1)

As with the discussion of the Law, Matthew begins by articulating basic principles for worship and then giving specific examples. The principle that is to guide Christian worship is marked by singular simplicity. For the followers of Jesus, worship is to be directed toward God with no concern for human respect or approval. Worship with an eye to human interest has no value before God. This principle deals not only with the direction of worship, but also with its goal. The first of the Ten Commandments is to worship God alone (Exod 20:3). Worship that is concerned for human praise not only detracts from proper worship; it also runs the risk of idolatry—worshiping something other than God. For life in the Kingdom, worship is to have a singular focus in God.

Examples of Worship
(6:2-34)

As with the discussion of the Law, examples are given concerning proper Christian worship. These include giving, prayer, fasting, and the danger of idolatry. As with the previous study, these examples do not provide a list covering every aspect of worship. Every detail of issues such as prayer is not addressed. The aim here is not to cover every possible technicality, but to provide principles and patterns to guide and inspire Christian worship. As with the discussion on Law, these patterns belong to life in the Kingdom: these values are to be lived out by the transformed individual and by Christian communities. Nonetheless these examples also speak to those not yet in the Kingdom and exert God's claim upon the world.

Giving
(6:2-4)

The principle that worship should be singularly focused on God is demonstrated in the matter of giving. Jesus rejects the giving of alms that sounds a trumpet and calls attention to itself (v. 2). The Greek term from which we get "hypocrite" means "actor." Jesus rejects piety that is nothing more than play acting. Such action may be praised by others, but it deserves no further attention. This is emphasized through the strong language used here: "Amen, I say to you . . ." (v. 2). Jesus demands a better way. He uses a colorful image to press home the point of pure giving: do not let the left hand know what the right hand is giving. This secretiveness is technically impossible, since our brain keeps track of both left and right, but the point of the image remains. Clarence Jordan offers another interpretation: reach into the pocket or purse and take out what you have. Do not then use the other hand to pick out a few coins, but give the whole handful![1] However we read this image, the point is clear: followers of Jesus are to give freely out of love for God and not to be seen by others. This instruction ends with a theological focus. Those who give in this way will be seen and rewarded by God (v. 4). This pattern of giving is to mark the worship of those in the Kingdom.

Prayer
(6:5-15)

Prayer is a central element in almost all religious experience. This was true of Judaism, and it is true of the followers of Jesus. But Jesus demands a different kind of prayer life.

The instruction on prayer follows the pattern of that on giving. Jesus forbids prayers that are given with an eye toward public approval. Thus, the desire to be seen as one who prays is excluded. Such prayers are hypocritical and have no further benefit. Jesus again brings home this point through a stark formula: "Amen, I say to you . . ." (v. 5). Jesus demands a higher righteousness. As with giving, Jesus tells his disciples to pray in secret so that God alone will be the focus of prayer. The theological perspective is again held in view: God is the one who will hear such prayers, and God is the one who will reward this worship.

Further instructions are given on the role of prayer in the life of the Kingdom (vv. 6-8). Babbling on and piling up many words are forbidden. Prayer is not a tool for public show, and it is not a way of convincing God. Frank Stagg makes this point:

> It is not that God needs to be asked but that we need to ask. Prayer is communion with God in which we are brought into new relationships and new attitudes, thus opening the way for blessings which God already purposed to impart.[2]

Jesus insists that God, as our Parent, already knows our needs. Prayer is not a means of informing God about us, but a way of opening ourselves to the God who is waiting to hear from us!

Jesus then provides an example of how disciples should pray (vv. 9-13). The lines of this simple prayer embody the demands of life in the Kingdom. The Disciples' Prayer opens with the recognition that God stands behind all of our existence as the ruler of the universe. Not our religious activities but the sovereignty of God stands as the basis of prayer and faith. Echoing the larger message of Jesus, disciples are reminded that the God who is sovereign over the heavens can be known to believers as the gracious Father. It is the believer's response to this gracious Parent that properly motivates and guides prayer.

With the recognition that God the gracious Parent stands behind our praying, Christian prayer receives new status and motivation. Personal and material concerns fall aside, and the disciple asks first for the realization of Kingdom values. "Let God's name be sacred" is the first request, echoing the third commandment (Exod 20:7). "Let your kingdom come," the disciple prays, echoing the proclamation of Jesus (Matt 4:17). In a parallel thought the believer prays, "Let your will be done on earth as it is in heaven." This is the prayer Jesus prays in Gethsemane (26:42) just before his death. While the coming of God's reign was often seen as a future event by Jewish worshipers, Jesus did not overlook its impact on the present. According to Eduard Schweizer, "Jesus thinks first from the point of the coming God and the coming reign and from this viewpoint lets light fall upon the present."[3] In reality all three requests belong together: proper reverence is given to God's name when God's reign becomes reality among humans. The values of the Kingdom are to dominate the prayer life of Jesus' followers. When these values are given priority, other concerns fall into place.

Only after the role of the Kingdom is addressed do personal and material concerns come into focus (6:11). Even these receive new perspective in light of God's reign. Bread enough for today is requested by the disciple. There is no thought here of an investment portfolio or a retirement plan; the disciple wants provision to carry out the tasks of this day.

The prayer for forgiveness (v. 12) confirms the pattern of correlation or correspondence that lies at the heart of the Sermon. Believers can ask to be forgiven, even as they forgive others. This is not a strict legal equation such as "one who forgives seven times can be forgiven seven times." Such an equation would depend upon the achievement of the believer rather than upon God's mercy. What is stated here is a matter of connectedness. Those who have experienced God's forgiveness will be forgiving; those who expect to be forgiven must be forgiving. Here is the responsive grace ethic of the Sermon: Jesus' radical demands are based upon God's extraordinary grace. We can expect forgiveness from God because God has become our Parent; God can expect forgiveness from us for others because we have become God's children. Anything less would be inconsistent and hypocritical. The problem is not with God, but with us. As Frank Stagg notes,

> It is not that God is unwilling to forgive the unforgiving but that the condition of the unforgiving is such that they are incapable of receiving forgiveness. When a door is closed, it is closed from both sides. What blocks the flow of mercy or forgiveness *from* us blocks its flow *to* us.[4]

Thus, God's forgiveness has initiated a stream of mercy that flows through the disciple into the world. Believers are to pray in view of this extraordinary stream of grace.

The final lines of the prayer (v. 13) are marching orders for the daily work of the Kingdom. Disciples are to pray that God will lead them away from temptation and will deliver them from the power of the evil one. The way of righteousness is to be pursued with foresight and wisdom, but it also depends upon the guiding mercies of God for each day's journey.[5]

It is important to note that Jesus directs the prayer life of disciples not toward himself, even as the risen Lord, but toward the Heavenly Father. The central tenet of the Old Testament and of Jewish faith—there is one God, and God alone is to be worshiped—is confirmed in the prayer life of Jesus and in his instructions for disciples. As Christians, we continue to pray this prayer to God because Jesus has taught us to do so.

One aspect of the Disciples' Prayer is given further emphasis (vv. 14-15). The correspondence of forgiveness is confirmed through a parallel statement that emphasizes first the positive, then the negative. Those who are forgiving toward others keep open the channel of God's forgiveness; those who refuse to forgive others also shut themselves off from God's forgiveness. This is no "tit-for-tat" equation, but a statement of consistency and coherence. Those who have experienced God's mercy will be merciful; failure to forgive bears witness to the fact that one has not yet understood and experienced the fullness of God's forgiveness. This radical demand for forgiveness is rooted in the extraordinary depth of God's patience and mercy.

Thus, the prayer life of the disciple is not to be guided by the notice or approval or concerns of human observers. It is to be guided instead by the overwhelming presence of God. This God who is sovereign over all of creation approaches us as a merciful Parent. The central concern of the disciple is to honor God and to see God's reign become reality in our world. Daily provision and guidance will be provided for this task.

This life of prayer is no retreat from the world, but a prelude to bold advance. The disciple is to emerge from prayer stripped of obsession with possessions and the collecting of things. The disciple is to emerge from prayer with a burning desire to see God's reign realized in the experience of daily life. Most of all, the disciple is to emerge from prayer armed with the power of unlimited forgiveness—a power rooted in the prior experience of God's mercy. Armed with the strength of unbounded forgiveness, the individual Christian and the believing community can be sent forth on a daily journey to change the world. Such is the power of prayer in the life of the Kingdom!

Fasting
(6:16-18)

Fasting was a part of the worship of Israel, continued into the life of the early church, and remains an important part of worship for many Christians today. Jesus assumes that his followers will continue the practice of fasting they learned from Judaism. He insists, however, on a different motivation and quality for this form of worship.

In a pattern almost identical to the teaching on giving and prayer, Jesus insists that his followers not fast to be seen by others. The stark "Amen, I say to you . . ." is repeated, indicating that fasting for show has no further reward. There is a catchy play on words in verse 16: Hypocrites put on sad looks and disfigure their faces when they fast to be noticed by others. The term for disfiguring the face means "to hide from sight" or "to render unrecognizable." Thus, these religious performers make their normal countenance unrecognizable in order to be recognized by others! This colorful language points to the empty nature of such worship. Jesus demands more. Those fasting with integrity should keep up a normal appearance before others. God will observe this quiet, sincere worship and will provide its proper reward. As with giving and praying, so with fasting: God is to be the only true observer and the only true object of our worship. The way of the Kingdom demands no less.

The Danger of Idolatry
(6:19-34)

The final and most extensive discussion on worship concerns the question of idolatry. This concern would be central for Matthew's audience, since it is likely that most of them came from a Jewish background. In the first of the Ten Commandments God insists that "you shall have no other gods before me" (Exod 20:3). The third commandment extends this to say "You shall make for yourself no idol" (v. 4). Thus, worshiping God alone and avoiding every form of idolatry lie at the heart of Old Testament faith. Jesus confirms this unique faithfulness to God in his own life and worship, and he passes these demands along to his disciples.

Modern Christians often think of wooden or clay or stone statues when they read this verse. Since few modern cultures use such objects, the command may appear simple and somewhat outdated. In contrast to this perception Jesus presents a radically different understanding of idolatry that has direct relevance for modern life.

The Sermon deals first with the question of personal possessions, which it describes as treasures (6:19-21). Parallel commands contrast earthly and heavenly treasures: earthly things may be devoured by moths and rust, while heavenly treasures cannot. Thieves can take away the earthly but not the heavenly. Therefore, Jesus commands his followers to store up their treasures in heaven.

Thus far the command is one of common sense—one should invest in that which endures. The final proverb (v. 21) moves beyond the realm of common sense to articulate an ethical principal at the foundation of human behavior: where your treasure is, there shall be also your heart. Consequently the ethic of Jesus is more concerned for the human heart than for the terms of investment. As Frank Stagg notes, Jesus was "both deeply concerned that people have the material necessities of life and that they be free from the tyranny of things."[6]

Those whose lives are wrapped up in a home or a piece of land or a stock portfolio may lose it all. When the market fails, they lose not only their investment, but also their sense of direction and identity. Some turn to crime when their investments fail, and some commit suicide. All of this confirms the observation of Jesus that treasures become a matter of the heart. Investing in heavenly treasure thus becomes far more than a matter of wise investment; it touches precisely upon the issue of idolatry. If one's treasure and one's heart belong to the bank, then the bank becomes an idol. If one's heart is on the golf course, then the game becomes an idol. Whenever life gathers around an object or a focus other than God, then the danger of idolatry lies close at hand.

Jesus insists that his followers solve this problem from the outset by making heavenly treasures the focus of their lives. This is not only wise, but also directs disciples away from the dangers of idolatry. But what does it mean to have heavenly treasure? We should not reduce this command to a few spiritual feelings or to some mystical realm. In the Gospel of Matthew heaven is God's domain. God's Kingdom is thus the Kingdom of Heaven. God is described as the Heavenly

Father. In Matthew's world view heavenly treasure and heavenly focus point to the sovereignty of God. Thus, to have heavenly treasure is to enjoy the richness of life under God's reign; it is to enjoy the righteousness and the right relationships that accompany life in the Kingdom.

This singular focus that leads one away from idolatry is sketched through a second image in verses 22-23. Jesus again employs a word of common sense: the focus of one's eyes affects functions of the entire person. Clear focus allows one to carry out normal functions with dexterity and precision—eating, walking, working. Similarly, double vision or clouded vision affects the whole person and all of that person's activities. So it is with the spiritual life. One who tries to live with an eye to both God and worldly values is bound to stumble. The whole equilibrium of life stands in danger. Even as the heart and its treasures are to belong uniquely to God, so the life of the disciple is to find its sole focus in the sovereignty of God. This image, like the image of treasure, directs the disciple away from the dangers of idolatry.

These images are confirmed in a third portrait drawn from everyday life (v. 24). Even as one cannot serve two earthly lords at the same time, so a disciple is unable to serve two lords. Such a person would have divided loyalty and would ultimately experience a divided life. The final proverb makes it clear that the issue of idolatry is still central: one cannot serve both God and earthly goods. One who chooses earthly goods will do so with the heart, and the danger of idolatry becomes imminent. Such a divided focus affects the whole life of the person. In order to remain free from every form of idolatry, God alone must have claim upon the life and the desire of the disciple. This demand is central to the invitation to come wholly under the reign of God. Thus, life in the Kingdom demands the higher righteousness that fulfills the first commandment: "You shall have no other gods before me" (Exod 20:3).

The whole issue of idolatry boils down to the question of priorities. This central concern is addressed in 6:25-34. This discussion leads to a stunning conclusion in verses 33-34: seek the righteousness of God's Kingdom for today; all else is secondary. The whole discussion of 6:25-34 leads up to and supports this conclusion.

Human anxiety is contrasted to the equilibrium of the natural order through two different lines of comparison. While humans worry about food and drink and clothing, the birds of the air are fed by the Heavenly Parent (vv. 25-26). Human worry is not able to add a minute or a centimeter to human life (indeed, science teaches us that anxiety takes away from both the quality and the quantity of life!). In contrast to the futility of human anxiety, the flowers of the field stand clothed by God in unsurpassable beauty (vv. 28-29). The point of these comparisons is twofold: human anxiety is not productive, and God's care for humans surpasses the wonder of the created order. This is confirmed in verses 31-32: human worry over food, drink, and clothing should be subsumed by the disciple's trust in God. Before we pray and before we worry, the God who clothed and fed the creation stands waiting for us. The extravagant grace, beauty, and nourishment displayed throughout nature is available for those who call upon God.

In view of this wondrously available grace it would be idolatry to allow any concern, desire, or need to shift our focus from the Heavenly Parent. God seeks to reign in lives free from anxiety, greed, and idolatry. Thus, the discussion on idolatry reaches its climax in the command of verses 33-34. This command defines both the focus and the reach that are to occupy the life of the disciple. The reign of God is to provide the singular focus for the life of the disciple, and the task of today is to fill the disciple's agenda. Other concerns are secondary; other days have too much to carry. For today, the follower of Jesus is called to give singular focus and allegiance to the work of the Kingdom. This commitment frees the disciple from the dangers of idolatry and provides the purest form of worship. Here is the higher righteousness that Jesus commands.

Conclusion

The instructions in Matthew 6:1-34 set forth new patterns of worship to be practiced by those in the Kingdom of God. These patterns obviously address the failures Jesus observed in the Jewish worship of his own day. They also reflect the concern of Matthew to establish authentic patterns of worship over against the fallen Temple and the hostile synagogue of his own day. Nonetheless the patterns found in Matthew 6:1-34 can give new focus and guidance to our own practice of worship.

As with other parts of the Sermon, this discussion does not cover every aspect of worship (nothing is said of music, for example). Nor does this discussion claim to cover every detail of any one aspect of worship. What these patterns do provide is a pattern for worship that demands a singular focus on God and the consistent practice of righteousness within the Kingdom. The singular focus of life under the reign of God will be reflected in the worship practices of the disciple and the believing community: in giving, in prayer, in fasting, and in rejection of every threat of idolatry. Practiced solely for God and focused distinctly upon God, this worship reflects the higher righteousness that marks life in the Kingdom.

Discussion Questions

Engaging the Text

1. What is the most important principle guiding proper worship?
2. Why do you think the instructions on worship in the Sermon draw so frequently upon the Ten Commandments?
3. Why do you think Jesus used so many images from everyday life?
4. Why do you think the Disciples' Prayer has been so widely used in the church?
5. In what ways are these instructions on worship negative? What are their positive aspects?

For Further Reflection

1. "It is better not to give at all than to give for the wrong reason." Do you agree? Why or why not?
2. "Prayer changes things." Do you agree? Why or why not? If so, what precisely does prayer change?
3. What is the greatest potential idol in modern culture? In the church? In your own life?
4. What role should fasting play in Christian worship today?
5. What role should nature play in our worship? What role should human creativity play? Should art, music, literature, poetry, and dance be used in worship?

Notes

[1] Clarence Jordan, *Sermon on the Mount*, rev. ed. (Valley Forge PA: Judson Press, 1993) 54.

[2] Frank Stagg, "Matthew," in *Broadman Bible Commentary*, ed. C. Allen (Nashville: Broadman Press, 1969) 115.

[3] Eduard Schweizer, *Die Bergpredigt* (Gottingen: Vandenhoeck & Ruprecht, 1982) 71.

[4] Stagg, 116.

[5] Many early texts of Matthew's Gospel conclude the prayer at this point. Others go on to include the familiar benediction, "For yours is the Kingdom and the power and the glory forever." Some texts include a different benediction: "Because yours is the Kingdom of the Father and of the Son and of the Holy Spirit forever. Amen." These benedictions may be later additions drawn from Christian worship that confirm the believer's assent to the prayer. These benedictions each echo the opening lines of the prayer: "Your Kingdom come . . . ." These different texts show that the Disciples' Prayer was used widely and frequently in the early church.

[6] Stagg, 117.

The Kingdom Lifestyle and Others

(Matt 7:1-6)

One of the most important tests of any religious experience is the way it leads its adherent to treat others. In the Old Testament, for example, God's promise of love to Israel formed the basis for a detailed code of behavior. At the center of this ethical code was instruction in how to treat others justly. This Old Testament pattern is central to the ethics of Jesus and to his instructions for disciples. How one treats others is a key element for participation in the Kingdom of God. While this concern has emerged in the midst of various other discussions, Matthew 7:1-6 speaks directly to this issue.

Judging Others
(7:1-5)

As with other lessons, the instruction on judging employs a principle followed by an illustration. The correlation we met in other parts of the Sermon is here set in wholly negative terms: "do not judge, lest you be judged" (v. 1). Thus, a stark warning is posed against all who would set themselves as judge over others, yet fail to meet their own standards. Jesus obviously has in mind some religious leaders of his own day, and Matthew likely finds this warning relevant to his own situation.

The correlation of judging and being judged extends also to the degree of judgment: those who judge others will be judged by their own measures. The meter of verse 2 is rhythmic and alliterative: "Because in what judgment you judge you shall be judged, and in what measure you measure you shall be measured." Behind this colorful language is the demand for consistency. Every form of hypocrisy must be avoided, for the judge will be judged with his/her own judgment. Perhaps there is a hidden barb here: the one who judges others will be judged by God! As Ulrich Luz notes, "The Kingdom of God is coming; there must in principle be an end to the judging of human beings by others."[1] Jesus thus insists that the hypocrisy so endemic to religious folks has no place in the Kingdom.

This principle is illustrated through a humorous image (vv. 3-5). Two people have something in their eye: one a speck of dust, the other a wooden beam. With absurd irony the person with the beam tries to remove the speck from the other person. Religious hypocrisy is like that, Jesus says. Those most eager to judge are often those most in need of correction. The answer to this hypocrisy is a critical sense of self-judgment: deal first with your own obstacle, Jesus says, then you may deal with the other person. Frank Stagg puts it this way:

> Only after one has known the shame or agony of coming under judgment and of having the log removed from his own eye will he understand the need and the feeling of the brother. Only then can he see clearly to take the speck from his brother's eye.[2]

This comical image of irony and reversal proves to be entertaining, but it also contains extraordinary wisdom. Such stories typify the way Jesus taught.

Discretion
(7:6)

The illustration in verses 3-5 seems to leave open the possibility of some discriminating judgment. The saying in verse 6 takes up this possibility. Once again using colorful images from everyday life, this saying warns against throwing precious things away. There is a wordplay behind this saying. In Aramaic the word for holy things is very similar to the word for pearls, creating a rhythmic parallelism. The sense of this saying is clear: spend your resources wisely. There are times and places where our efforts offer no hope of success.

An instance from early church history might illustrate this point. Those who died as martyrs for their Christian faith were held in high esteem among early believers. Recognizing this, the young Origen

(185–253 CE) was intent upon throwing himself before the Romans and becoming a martyr for the cause of Christ. His mother exercised a more prudent wisdom: she hid her son's clothes, knowing he would be too embarrassed to confront the Romans naked. Origen lived to become an important leader in the early church. A number of his students became Christian martyrs, and Origen himself died as a result of persecution. This discriminating judgment that chooses the proper time for witness and sacrifice should mark the life of the disciple under God's reign.

Conclusion

Life under God's reign requires that one be properly related to God through worship. This relationship extends into the social relations of the disciple. One who no longer worships to be seen by others will put aside the urge to judge others. This unique focus upon God prevents both idolatry and religious hypocrisy. To the degree that judgment is exercised, it must begin with a critical self-evaluation. Further, disciples should learn to judge the times and to choose well the place for witness and sacrifice. In their interactions with others, Christians should be blinded neither by hypocrisy nor by naiveté.

This extension of the ethics of the Kingdom into the social realm has an important impact. First, barriers that block the way between disciples and non-Christians are removed. The follower of Jesus can no longer approach others with a sense of superiority and condemnation. The haughty religious hypocrisy that has kept so many out of the church is blocked by the command to first exercise critical self-judgment. Those busy with self-judgment will have little time or energy left to consider the faults of others!

As a consequence, a renewed path of witness may be opened into the lives of those around us. When judgment of others has ceased, the disciple may then become a channel through which others experience the extraordinary grace of God. Only when the stream of judgment and condemnation is blocked can God's mercy flow through the disciple to claim others for the Kingdom. Thus, the command "Do not judge" becomes an effective means of evangelism. The compassionate Christian community that offers nonjudgmental acceptance will draw others into the Kingdom. When all forms of hypocritical judgment have ceased, channels of grace are opened through which the world may experience the mercy and forgiveness of God. In this way criticism is replaced by compassion, and perhaps by conversion! This noncritical engagement of others belongs to the way of the Kingdom.

Discussion Questions

Engaging the Text

1. Why is it so important that Jesus' followers stop judging others? How can judging others affect our relationship with God? How can it affect our relationship with other people?
2. How do you think the story of the log and the speck would impact those listening to Jesus? Would it invoke laughter? Thoughtfulness? Anger?
3. Does the language of Matthew 7:6 sound harsh to you? What are some ways in which this saying might be misused?

For Further Reflection

1. Is judgment of others always wrong? Should a jury judge a criminal? Should we exercise judgment in choosing a spouse? Is some form of judgment necessary? If so, what is the proper form of judgment?
2. Having read Matthew 7:3-5, can you think of other illustrations that make the same point?
3. Can judgment ever have a place in the church? If so, in what form and for what purposes?

4. Can you think of situations from your own experience that illustrate the point of Matthew 7:6?
5. What type of people might be attracted to the church by a non-judgmental approach?
6. Can you remember an instance in which you experienced the non-judgmental engagement of a Christian? How did this affect you?

Notes

[1] Ulrich Luz, *Matthew: A Continental Commentary* (Minneapolis: Fortress Press, 1992) 416.

[2] Frank Stagg, "Matthew," in *Broadman Bible Commentary*, ed. C. Allen (Nashville: Broadman Press, 1969) 120.

The Kingdom Lifestyle and Self

(Matt 7:7-27)

The last major section of the Sermon on the Mount deals with the Kingdom and the life of the individual. While life under God's Reign is a call to community with crucial social consequences, this lifestyle ultimately hinges upon the free choice and faithful activity of the individual.

The Principle of Availability
(7:7-14)

The principle outlined in Matthew 7:7-14 provides the key for understanding the Sermon on the Mount. Put simply, the principle is this: God is available to us as a gracious Parent, and this relationship guides our treatment of others.

God's Availability
(7:7-12)

Those who listen to the Sermon are invited to ask, to seek, and to knock in their time of need (v. 7). Accompanying this invitation is the assurance that one who asks will receive, that one who seeks will find, that the door will be opened to one who knocks (v. 8). Certainly the invitation and assurance seem optimistic in a world such as ours. How much more unrealistic it must have seemed in Jesus' day when Rome held the people as economic and political captives and corrupt religious leaders held sway over the people! Jesus' audience was accustomed to having things taken away by deceit and violence. How strange this invitation to ask and this assurance to receive must have seemed to them.

Jesus' invitation and assurance are not built upon a logical base, but on a theological base. They are not grounded in the goodness of humans or in their systems of government and economics; they are rooted in the nature and activity of God. Jesus' listeners can boldly seek with the expectation of finding because God hears their requests.

But how does this differ from the religious expectations that preceded Jesus and the religious teachings of other traditions? The key difference in the teaching of Jesus is his understanding of God. God is not a distant despot to be appeased with strict behavior or sacrificial payments. Jesus presents God as the gracious Parent who stands nearby attending to the needs of each child.

This imagery is confirmed through an argument from the lesser to the greater (vv. 9-11). The example of a caring human parent is invoked: if a child asks for food, no caring parent would deny or deceive the child. Child abuse is prevalent in today's world, and exceptions could obviously be cited. Nonetheless the point stands, especially within the ethical world of Jewish piety that Jesus addresses: even bad people know how to show compassion for their children's needs. The point of this comparison is reached in verse 11: if human parents show such compassion, how much more so the Heavenly Father! Behind all the requests and demands of the Sermon stands the compassionate image of God, the Heavenly Parent who attends the needs of each person. This is the key to understanding the Sermon on the Mount and the religion of Jesus: God is available as a gracious Parent to those who ask, seek, or knock.

Only when God's surprising availability and grace are experienced can one understand the command that follows: do to others as you want done to you (v. 12). It is important to perceive that the gift of God's mercy precedes and enables this command and all of the demands of the Sermon. The waiting presence of God is the foundational act of grace that precedes all God's demands. Thus, the believer is to practice a responsive grace ethic: the mercy experienced in one's relationship to God is to be practiced in one's relationship to others.

Failure to practice this responsive mercy is to cheapen and to deny the grace of God. For many Christians, the term "grace" invokes images of salvation without any connection to good works. Thus, grace may be misunderstood to mean salvation without discipleship.

It is precisely this false view of salvation that Dietrich Bonhoeffer, a German pastor who resisted Hitler's power, labeled as "cheap grace." He defined cheap grace as:

> The preaching of forgiveness without requiring repentance, baptism without church discipline, communion without confession, absolution without personal confession. Cheap grace is grace without discipleship, grace without the cross, grace without Jesus Christ, living and incarnate.[1]

Bonhoeffer believed that "the word of cheap grace has been the ruin of more Christians than any other commandment of works."[2]

Properly understood, salvation includes both justification (being made right with God) and discipleship. This union of justification and discipleship Bonhoeffer labeled as "costly grace":

> Costly grace is the treasure hidden in the field; for the sake of it a man will gladly go and sell all that he has. It is the pearl of great price to buy which the merchant will sell all his goods. It is the kingly rule of Christ, for whose sake a man will pluck out the eye which causes him to stumble, it is the call of Jesus Christ at which the disciple leaves his net and follows him.[3]

As the Sermon shows, the call to experience the extraordinary grace of God means more than personal forgiveness of sin. Rooted in this offer of forgiveness is the call to discipleship through service and suffering. This is, in the words of Frank Stagg, the "gift and demand" of the gospel.[4] Consequently, the claim to be saved by God's grace of necessity implies the call to discipleship. Bonhoeffer emphasized this point:

> The only man who has the right to say that he is justified by grace alone is the man who has left all to follow Christ. Such a man knows that the call to discipleship is a gift of grace, and that the call is inseparable from the grace.[5]

Thus, the extraordinary grace of God unleashes in the disciple an ethic of responsive grace acted out toward others.

This principle is relevant for the "Golden Rule" of verse 12. There is a certain logic or common sense to the command to treat others as you wish to be treated. Indeed, the command to not do to others what you do not want done to yourself may be found in various religious texts. For example, the Jewish book of Tobit commands: "What you hate, do not do to anyone" (Tobit 4:15). Even the positive form of the command may have been in use prior to Jesus' time. In the book of Sirach, a Jewish writing dating from about 180 BCE, the command is given to "judge your neighbor's feelings by your own, and in every matter be thoughtful" (Sirach 31:15).

Indeed, the world would be a better, wiser place if individuals considered their actions and acted toward others in the way they themselves wish to be treated. This logic soon breaks down, however. Treating a dictator with compassion does not guarantee reform, and treating an opponent with mercy does not always prevent injustice. This logic can only hope that others will respond in kind.

The command of Jesus contains this common wisdom, but it also exceeds it. Jesus presents no ideal program in which treating despots kindly will guarantee their transformation. Rather, the Golden Rule belongs uniquely to life in the Kingdom. As Frank Stagg says,

> The Golden Rule presupposes discipleship, submission to the rule of God. It is not a sufficient rule for everyone. In a pagan life the "rule" would be experienced in terms of pagan values, for pagan wishes come from a pagan heart. The intention of the Golden Rule, presupposing discipleship, is that one is to be concerned for the other person's good as for his own.[6]

What Jesus does present in these verses is a way in which his followers can insure that their actions are just and initiate a pattern of reconciliation. The action of a believer is never to be determined by what someone else has done to us or even by the circumstances around us. Disciples are not to be content to repay the kindness or hostility of others—anyone can do this. The action of disciples is not to be reactive, but proactive; they are to treat others as they wish others would treat them.

This command does not represent an idealism without foundations, nor does it present a naive understanding of human nature. In Jesus' teaching this command is rooted in the prior mercy of God. Disciples have a clear model for how they wish to be treated. They have learned that God is like a Heavenly Parent who hears the needs of each child. They have learned to ask, seek, and knock, knowing that God awaits with mercy and kindness and forgiveness. This experience of God's grace creates in the believer a new perception of what it means to be human.

This is how people wish to be treated, and this is how disciples are to treat others. Regardless of how others have treated us, believers are to respond to others with the same grace and kindness we have experienced from God. Thus, the hope of a better world is not rooted in some far-off utopia or in a naive view of human nature; it is grounded instead in the new reality created by God. The Kingdom of God is a new reality established in the life of the believer through the grace of God, and the extension of this reality into the life of others provides the primary task of the disciple.

This is the central ethical command in the teaching of Jesus. This principle also provides the key to understanding the various components of the Sermon on the Mount. Each blessing and each demand placed upon the life of the believer is to be understood against this backdrop. Those who enter the Kingdom do so because of the extraordinary mercy of God; the radical demands placed upon the disciple are rooted in this experience of God. The Sermon thus offers a responsive grace ethic: those who have experienced God's mercy and entered the Kingdom are to respond to others with this same grace.

This responsive grace ethic clarifies the stringent and unconditional demands for obedience imposed by the Sermon. According to Joachim Jeremias, "Only if we begin with the greatness of the gift of God can we really understand the heavy nature of the demand which Jesus makes."[7]

Understanding the Sermon as a responsive grace ethic also explains why it does not provide a complete list of rules, but a working model for discipleship. Jeremias put it this way:

> What Jesus teaches in the sayings collected in the Sermon on the Mount is not a complete regulation of the life of the disciples, and it is not intended to be; rather, what is here taught is symptoms, signs, examples, of what it means when the kingdom of God breaks into the world which is still under sin, death, and the devil.[8]

It is the task of the disciple and of the believing community to apply and extend this model to address the needs of daily life.

Those who have experienced God's mercy and entered the Kingdom are to respond to others with this same grace. Jesus confirms the centrality of this command, insisting that it sums up the Law and the Prophets (v. 12). This, Jesus says, is what the Bible is all about. Obviously this one command cannot say everything, and it cannot deal with every situation. What it does is to articulate the very heart of God's purposes. This is what God was doing through the Law; this is what the prophets were announcing. This is what happens when God rules in a human life. The reign of God is realized when the disciple who has experienced God's mercy responds to others with that same mercy. This is the fulfillment of the hopes and demands of the Old Testament. This is the radically new and transforming reality brought to pass in the Kingdom of God.

The believer is to be reminded that this is not merely a matter of attitude such as "think kindly of all people." This command centers on "doing." Disciples are to do to others as they wish to have done to them. Discipleship is thus to be lived out in real deeds that impact the lives of other human beings.

Thus, the radical availability of God to those who ask inspires the ethical conduct of those who have entered the Kingdom. Not external circumstances, and certainly not the behavior of others, are to guide the conduct of the disciple. The follower of Jesus is to be guided by the ideal of treating others as one wishes to be treated. This ideal has concrete grounding in the disciple's own dealings with God. One who has experienced God's mercy has been liberated from the demands of circumstance and recompense to extend the hand of mercy and compassion to others. This is the fulfillment of biblical faith; this is the way of the Kingdom.

Becoming Available to God
(7:13-14)

Corresponding to the radical availability of God is the demand that disciples make their lives wholly available to God. This command is articulated in the lesson of the gate and the road (vv. 12-13). Two contrasting ways of life are presented: one leads to death and one to life. The broad gate and the easy road are traveled by many, but this is the way of destruction. The narrow gate and the difficult road are chosen by few, but this is the way of life.

This lesson provides crucial images for life in the Kingdom. First, the way of the Kingdom is marked by difficulty: the gate is narrow, and the way is difficult. For many, the mention of grace invokes images of luxury and laxity, but the grace of the Sermon is a demanding grace fraught with difficulty. Life under God's reign demands perfection of the disciple (v. 48) and offers the promise of persecution and abuse (vv. 11-12). The ethics of the Kingdom are not the easy way or the simple way, but they are the way to life.

Second, life in the Kingdom is not just a beginning; it is a journey. Both conversion and consistency are emphasized. There is a gate that must be entered, and there is a road that must be trod. Life under God's reign begins with the personal experience of conversion in which one comes, through repentance, under the mercy and forgiveness of God. This experience must then be extended into the daily journey of discipleship. Thus, the experience of the Kingdom is both a gate and a way; it is a new beginning and a daily journey.

In this way Matthew 7:7-12 points to the values and demands that lie at the heart of the Sermon. At the center of Jesus' message is his radical understanding of God as the waiting Father. Not only the experience of grace, but also the stringent demands of discipleship are rooted in this understanding of God. One who experiences the gift of God's grace enters under God's rule and comes under the radical demands of discipleship. The new reality created in the disciple's relationship with God motivates and guides the conduct of the disciple in relation to others. The God who has become so radically available to us demands a corresponding availability from disciples; they must choose the narrow gate and walk the difficult way. Here is the key principle that energizes life under the rule of God.

The Principle of Consistency
(7:15-23)

Even as life in the Kingdom originates with God's availability, so it must be marked by the disciple's consistency. The harshest criticism by Jesus was leveled against those who claim religious values but are inconsistent in their practice. These folks Jesus labeled as hypocrites. Matthew also knows of inconsistent religious leaders, and he warns his community against this danger. Such leaders are labeled as false prophets and compared to wolves in sheep's clothing (v. 15). The danger continues, and the warning is still valid!

A Tree and Its Fruit
(7:15-20)

Three different pictures illustrate the dangers of hypocrisy and call disciples to consistent practice of their faith. The first image is drawn from the world of horticulture: the fruit is consistent with the tree that bore it (vv. 16-20). We miss the point if we try to press this image into a scientific rule. For example, some thorny bushes produce excellent berries. Further, we do not usually think of plants as good or evil. All of this would miss the point of such illustrations. Jesus' use of horticultural images points the listener to a central truth and invites further reflection.

The point in Matthew 7:15-20 is the consistency between actions and the motivations that produce those actions. The consistency found in nature (briars produce briars, figs produce figs) models that of the ethical realm. Ultimately, the nature and value of a plant may be judged by the fruit it produces. So it is with ethical values: those who claim to represent morality and religion must consistently exhibit these values in their deeds. To do otherwise does not discredit religion; it discredits the one who thus claims to be religious. Religion that does not produce active righteousness is worthy of judgment and destruction (v. 19). This is the warning that Jesus issues in the Sermon and that Matthew emphasizes for his community: true religion can be tested by the ethical fruit it produces. This principle would be particularly relevant to Jewish listeners, for it echoes the central demands of the Old Testament.

A further claim is inherent in this image. Even as the production of fruit is a natural consequence of a plant's identity, so the life of righteousness is a natural result of discipleship. The ethical practices of Christians are not to be seen as extraordinary works, and they are not to be limited to a select few. Discipleship is not the product of unusual motivation or hyperactivity; it is the natural outflow of a life that has come under the extraordinary grace of God's reign.

Thus, the follower of Jesus is instructed to test religious claims against the fruit they bear. Bad religion cannot produce good fruit, and authentic religious experience naturally produces good works. Active righteousness, consistently and naturally produced, marks the lifestyle of those who have entered into the reign of God.

Words and Lifestyle
(7:21)

The second lesson on consistency draws upon the connection between words and lifestyles. At the center of verse 21 is the early Christian confession that Jesus is Lord. It was this confession that distinguished the faith of Christians and made them vulnerable to persecution. Confessing Jesus as Lord could exclude one from the synagogue and result in death at the hands of the Romans. Thus, the confession that Jesus is Lord could be seen as the identifying trait of early Christianity.

Even this dramatic confession does not ensure that one is righteous. It is not the proper confession that ensure righteousness, but the proper practice. It is irrelevant to confess Jesus as Lord if one does not do the will of the Father whom Jesus proclaimed. Utter consistency is required of those who would enter the Kingdom. While confessions of faith have their place, they must be backed up by the consistent practice of God's will.

Deeds and Relationships
(7:22-23)

The final lesson on consistency reverses this pattern. A life of activity is no substitute for a personal relationship with Jesus. No list of human works and accomplishments can make one right before God. Paul discovered this through much struggle, and his pilgrimage was repeated in the experience of Martin Luther. Even the greatest of religious activity—proper confessions, prophecy, exorcisms, wonders—provide no substitute for saving faith. To address such claims, Jesus flashes forward to the day of judgment. In that day many will confess to know Jesus as Lord (v. 22). In reply, Jesus will confess, "I never knew you" (v. 23). In an ironic citation from the Old Testament, these busy people are condemned as "those working unlawful things." Thus, Jesus requires consistency between one's deeds and the faith that motivates those deeds. The Kingdom of God is not about busy religious activity; it is about transformed lives that confess Jesus' Lordship through word and deed. Here is the consistency that marks life under the rule of God.

The Picture of Life
(7:24-27)

Ultimately the values of the Kingdom are summarized in the story of two housebuilders. Like much of Jewish literature, this scene focuses on the difference between the wise person and the foolish person.[9] In this story the wise housebuilder constructs upon a strong, rocky foundation. The foolish housebuilder constructs on a foundation of sand. While the structures they build may appear of equal worth, they do not equally stand the test of the storm: the sandy foundation is quickly eroded and its superstructure destroyed.

This parable of wisdom applies equally to the life of faith. What distinguishes the faith of Christians from other religious experience? What distinguishes the activity of the church from that of other organizations concerned for human welfare? Perhaps the key lies in this story from Jesus. Life under God's rule means there is a vital connection between the foundation and the superstructure. Thus, Christian conversion and the life of discipleship are an inseparable unity. The wise person is one who builds consistently upon the strong foundation of Christian faith.

Jesus' story thus demands utter consistency between hearing and doing. It is not enough that one is moved by Jesus' words. It is not sufficient that Jesus' instructions lead to theological reflection. Casual acquaintance with the teaching of Jesus is not enough. Jesus demands both hearing and doing. Religious confession that does not produce active righteousness is empty. Social transformation that does not root in the experience of faith is incomplete. Jesus demands both faith and works, both hearing and doing. This wisdom and consistency mark the life of the disciple under the reign of God.

Conclusion

Thus, the final segment of the Sermon points to the transformation of the individual under the reign of God. The principle of availability (vv. 7-14) stands at the heart of the Sermon. Jesus presents God as the waiting Father who is radically available to each person. Those who experience this grace are to be gracious in their dealings with others. The life of the disciple is to be wholly and consistently open to God. The principle of consistency (vv. 15-23) demands a radical coherence between the confession and the practice of faith. The concluding lesson on housebuilding (vv. 24-27) calls for discipleship that combines word and deed, hearing and doing, in the living of Christian faith.

Thus, the call to the Kingdom is ultimately a call to personal conversion and transformation. This initial experience of God's grace is to be lived out through a life of consistent discipleship. The motivation for this lifestyle lies not in human potential or ambition, but in the experience of God's mercy. This transformation of the self is not limited, however, to the personal. The treatment of others with what they need rather than with what they expect or deserve moves the Kingdom values into the public forum. This social engagement by the transformed individual may have a stark impact upon other persons and eventually upon society and culture. The consistent righteousness practiced in the life of the disciple provides the most engaging witness to the Kingdom and the most productive hope for transformation of the world.

Discussion Questions

Engaging the Text

1. Why is the principle of God's availability so central to the Sermon?
2. What distinguishes Jesus' teachings from his Jewish predecessors? From his Jewish contemporaries? From other religious traditions?
3. The story of the two ways continued to be used in early Christian literature. Why do you think this lesson was so popular?

4. What is the relationship between wisdom and the way of the Kingdom? Is wisdom a good virtue? Is wisdom sufficient?
5. What value might these lessons have for a non-Christian?

For Further Reflection

1. Jesus spoke of God as the Heavenly Father. Is it appropriate for us to speak of God as Parent or as Mother? In what ways do parenting images help us to think of God? What are the limitations of such images?
2. Jesus warned against false prophets who do not bear good fruit. Do you know of such people today? How would you identify them?
3. Are there some people who follow Jesus by their actions although they do not confess Christian faith? Is there such a thing as a secret Christian or an anonymous Christian?
4. How does the transformation presented in these lessons specifically affect the life of an individual? A community? A political party? A nation?
5. Could you use the Sermon on the Mount to witness to a non-Christian? How would you begin?

Notes

[1] Dietrich Bonhoeffer, *The Cost of Discipleship* (New York: MacMillan, 1963) 47.
[2] Ibid., 59.
[3] Ibid., 47.
[4] Frank Stagg, "Matthew," in *Broadman Bible Commentary*, ed. C. Allen (Nashville: Broadman Press, 1969) 103.
[5] Bonhoeffer, 55.
[6] Stagg, 121.
[7] Joachim Jeremias, *The Sermon on the Mount*, tr. N. Perrin (Philadelphia: Fortress Press, 1963) 32.
[8] Ibid., 33.
[9] Examples of Jewish wisdom may be found in the Old Testament book of Proverbs and in Jewish literature such as the Wisdom of Solomon.

Conclusion

(Matt 7:28-29)

Matthew, who consistently organizes the sayings of Jesus into teaching units, provides a clear conclusion to the Sermon. This conclusion focuses on the audience (v. 28) and the Teacher (v. 29).

While the disciples were the primary audience of the Sermon, the presence of the crowd was noted in the introduction (5:1-2). In 7:28-29 the response of the crowd provides the conclusion to the Sermon. Matthew notes that the crowds are amazed at the teaching of Jesus, a description he borrows from the Gospel of Mark (1:22). While the Gospel of Mark usually associates such amazement with the miracles of Jesus, Matthew attaches the wonder of the crowds precisely to the words of Jesus. In this way Matthew emphasizes the authority of Jesus' teaching for both disciples and the world.

The amazement of the crowd shifts the focus to the second concern of Matthew's conclusion: the role of the Teacher. The source of the crowd's amazement is the teaching of Jesus. In particular they are amazed at the authority with which Jesus teaches. On the basis of this authority Matthew emphasizes the contrast between Jesus' teaching and that of the Jewish scribes.

Many scholars see here a clue to Matthew's audience and his wider purpose in presenting this material. Matthew seems eager to contrast the life of his own community with that of the synagogues that may have expelled these Christians. Matthew wants to make clear that the expelled Christians are no lawless band of unbelievers: they have in the teachings of Jesus an authoritative tradition that interprets and fulfills the Law of Moses. Matthew believes that the proper interpretation and application of God's Law is not found among the Pharisees such as those at Jamnia, but among those who heed the words of Jesus. For this reason Matthew places a similar summary at the end of each of five major discourses (speeches) in his Gospel (7:28; 11:1; 13:53; 19:1; 26:1).

For Matthew, the key example of this authority is to be found in the Sermon on the Mount. Matthew thus invites his own community to stand where the first crowds stood and to share their amazement at the authority of these words and of this Teacher. For all who would attend the words of the Sermon, this invitation is still valid.

✝ ✝ ✝

We have come to the end of our study of the Sermon. The following theses are presented as summary and focus of the issues raised by the Sermon. These propositions are intended to stir further reflection and response to the Sermon.

- The Sermon on the Mount belongs to the larger proclamation of the gospel message. It cannot be abstracted from its home in the teachings of Jesus and in the framework of the Gospel narratives. The Sermon cannot be reduced to a set of universal principles or a new list of rules; it belongs to the Christian message.

- The Sermon on the Mount is an extension and explication of Jesus' teaching on the Kingdom of God. Matthew makes this clear by his placement and arrangement of this material. To interpret the Sermon apart from this context is to do it violence. The Kingdom and the Sermon belong together.

- The Sermon on the Mount belongs to the larger context of Jewish faith. Its heritage lies in the Old Testament; its ethic and its piety draw deeply from Hebraic streams of tradition; its Teacher and its audience are faithful Jews; and its author (Matthew) stands within the Jewish tradition and is eager to demonstrate the faithfulness of Christianity to the Law and the Prophets.

- The concepts and demands of the Sermon claim to take up the traditions of Hebrew faith, but also to extend those traditions through a pattern of fulfillment. The Sermon aims for the intent of the Law and calls for the active righteousness demanded in the Law.

- Matthew has taken up the traditions of Jesus' teaching, but he has edited and applied them to the specific contours of his own community. The Christian community Matthew addresses is most likely composed of Christians with a Jewish background. The fall of the Temple and the expulsion of Christians from synagogues raise the need to clarify the identity and integrity of the Christian movement. Controversy with the Pharisees likely stands behind this presentation. Matthew thus presents Jesus and his teaching as the fulfillment of the Law and the Prophets and as the key to righteousness.

- The basic presupposition behind the Sermon and all of the teaching of Jesus is his unique perception of God. Jesus insists that God is like a Heavenly Parent—the Heavenly Father in the language of Jesus—who stands near to the needs of each child. To meet this Parent is to be confronted by extraordinary grace, mercy, and forgiveness. This mercy is available to all, regardless of race, sex, class, or religious standing.

- It is this experience of grace that stands behind all of the blessings and demands of the Sermon. The Blessings belong to this experience of God's mercy. The stringent measures and illogical behavior demanded of those who would follow Jesus are rooted in and motivated by the prior experience of God's grace. This responsive grace ethic provides the key to the Sermon on the Mount.

- The lifestyle described in the Sermon is not a comprehensive description, but a programmatic one. The examples of obedience sketched here must be extended and applied to each area of life by each individual believer and each Christian community.

- Entrance into the Kingdom demands personal transformation that is evidenced in a lifestyle of righteous deeds. This Kingdom lifestyle will be reflected in various arenas of personal life.

- The personal transformation portrayed in the Sermon must be lived out in the public arena. The transformed disciple is to actualize the new reality of the Kingdom in relationship with others, even one's enemies. The values of the Kingdom are to characterize the life of the Christian community as it lives within the world.

- Since the Sermon presents an ethic based upon personal religious experience and conversion, its values cannot be imposed from above by legal codes or constitutions. The ethics of the Kingdom remain forever the ethics of faith, not of coercion. Writing the Sermon on the Mount into the constitution of a nation or the charter of an international body does not insure its values. Christians cannot ask governments to impose Christian values on a pluralistic society. The church must work as a redemptive agent of change—as salt and light—that draws others to choose the values of the Kingdom.

- While the Sermon is an ethic rooted in personal conversion and transformation, its effects must be extended beyond personal concerns. Disciples are commanded to confront neighbors and enemies, nations and rulers, with the new reality of the Kingdom. This commitment helps the disciple to live justly in an unjust world. While this pattern of engagement does not guarantee a world of justice or peace or righteousness, it does confront the world with the values of the Kingdom. A new reality is modeled, and alternatives to violence, retribution, and destruction are articulated. In this way the world is confronted with the power of the meek, the merciful, the nonviolent, and the forgiving. The possibility and the claim of a new reality under the reign of God are modeled before the world in the life of faithful discipleship. This discipleship provides the most engaging witness and the most productive hope for transformation of the world.

- These patterns of engagement must be worked out and implemented anew in each generation. We can learn from our predecessors, but we cannot live in their times and places. The values of the Sermon and its engagement with the world must be transposed and translated for new times and places and peoples. The call of Jesus is never static; the task of discipleship must be learned afresh in each generation.

At the end of our reflection on the Sermon, one task remains. Those who hear the words of the Sermon are commanded to put them into practice. Hearing without doing is foolish and vain (7:24-27). The implementation of the Sermon on the Mount is the task given to each generation of Christians. It is a task to be fulfilled in new ways for changing times and places. That is the task before us. The Sermon on the Mount presents the possibilities and demands of the Kingdom. God and the world await our response.

Discussion Questions

Engaging the Text

1. What aspect of the Sermon do you find most comforting? What part do you find most disturbing?
2. What part of the Sermon is most relevant for your life? To what part is it the most difficult to relate?
3. In what ways do you think Matthew tailored his presentation of the Sermon to meet the needs of his audience? In what ways should we do this?
4. Which of the lessons from common life used in the Sermon made the most impact on you? Why?
5. What is the most important thing you have learned in your study of the Sermon?

For Further Reflection

1. How does the teaching authority of the Sermon compare with the teaching authority of religious leaders you know?
2. If taken seriously, what changes would the Sermon bring about in your life? In the church? In your community?
3. What types of non-Christians might find in the Sermon an attractive witness to Christian faith?
4. What is the major issue in the news this week? How does the Sermon speak to this issue?
5. Would you be willing to list specific acts you plan to do to carry out the demands of the Sermon? Would you be willing to write out a personal pledge to live under the demands of Jesus as presented in the Sermon?

The Sermon's Impact

Our interpretation of the Sermon on the Mount has centered around the original context of Jesus' teachings and upon their application within the community behind the Gospel of Matthew. We turn now to a more extended view of the impact of the Sermon.

The teachings of Jesus found in the Sermon on the Mount were passed on to successive generations and taken by Christians into new social and political contexts. These new times and places required that the words of the Sermon not only be preserved, but also be translated, interpreted, and applied in the light of their present situation. The early Christians behind the *Didache*, for example, lived about 90–120 CE. They were a minority cult in a world controlled by Hellenistic culture and Roman administration. In contrast, Chrysostom used the Sermon in a time when Christianity was tolerated by the Roman Empire (345–357 CE). Augustine wrote in the last days of the Roman Empire in North Africa (392–396 CE), and he feared that the Christian cultural synthesis was collapsing. These new times and places affected the way these Christians understood and applied the Sermon on the Mount.

This interpretive shift is not necessarily a loss that detracts from the original message of the Sermon. Since communication requires both a telling and a hearing, both sides of this conversation must be taken seriously. If the words of Jesus were to remain relevant, they had to be translated into new languages, they had to address new questions, and they had to be applied in the lives of a different community. The survival of the Sermon is testimony that Christians have allowed it to speak in new ways to the changing questions of human history.

We turn now to six historical groups or persons who were impacted deeply by the teachings of Jesus in the Sermon on the Mount. Certain lines of continuity may be observed between these people. Of greater interest will be the variety of ways in which these groups used the Sermon to address the critical issues of their era.

These studies are presented not simply out of historical interest; they are of greater interest as models of how different people have been influenced by the Sermon and have sought to apply its teachings to their age. No one of these patterns, not even that of Matthew's community, can tell us how we should interpret the Sermon and apply it to our times. These models are meant to be guides and catalysts that stir us to seek the wisdom of the Sermon for the questions and crises of our own age.

The Anabaptists

In all of Christian history the most dramatic attempt to implement the Sermon on the Mount may to be found among the Anabaptists. We shall look briefly at their origin and development, their application of the Sermon, and their continuing impact in modern society.

Origin and Development

The name Anabaptist, which comes from a term that means "to rebaptize," originated as a term of derision.[1] The Anabaptist movement arose first in the early 1500s among the followers of Ulrich Zwingli, the leader of the Protestant Reformation in Zürich, Switzerland. Soon after he was called to be the people's priest at the cathedral in Zürich, Zwingli initiated a number of reforms that led to the break with Catholicism, the first and most important of which was his turn to the scriptures.

Beginning on January 1, 1519, Zwingli stood daily in the cathedral to preach from the scriptures. In contrast to the Latin mass, he began by reading a few verses from the Gospel of Matthew in Greek or Latin, then translating them into Swiss German. Zwingli preached daily in the language of the people, something previously unknown.

Zwingli also initiated other reforms. Eventually the cathedral was stripped of its ornaments and images, priests gave up special clothing and were allowed to marry, and the mass was replaced by a simple liturgy of worship. Communion was celebrated as a simple meal that symbolized the presence of Christ among the people. Zwingli's reformation was an orderly and intellectual one, influenced by the growing intellectual enlightenment in Europe, especially by the humanistic teachings of Erasmus. Of particular importance was Zwingli's use of the Greek New Testament and his reading of the Church Fathers.

The first Anabaptist leaders were followers of Zwingli. Like Zwingli, they were educated. Initially a part of the Bible study movement sponsored by Zwingli, these students grew weary of his insistence that the reformation go forward only with the approval of the city council. When Zwingli, in deference to the city council, failed to carry through on his promise to abolish the mass by Christmas Day of 1523, his radical students committed themselves to move forward without his approval, or that of the city council.

While the central issue was the pace of the reform, the debate centered around the role of infant baptism. Rejecting infant baptism as unscriptural, a dozen people gathered at the home of Felix Mainz on January 21, 1525, in the shadow of the cathedral, to discuss the future of the movement. After a time of prayer, George Blaurock asked Conrad Grebel to baptize him. Blaurock then baptized the others. This act of conscience, carried out in defiance of both Zwingli and the city council, marked the beginning of the free church or believers' church tradition.

Persecution at the hands of the Protestant city government began within a month. When imprisonment proved ineffective, authorities began to hunt down and to execute Anabaptists. Bolt Eberle was executed in 1525 by Catholic authorities and thus became the first Protestant martyr. Felix Mainz was condemned by the Protestant city council of Zürich and was drowned in the Limmat River on January 5, 1527. Most, if not all, of the major leaders of the movement were dead within a few years.

This movement to restore a New Testament model for the church centered around baptism as a symbol of adult conversion spread quickly beyond Zürich. Over the next centuries Anabaptists were active in other parts of Switzerland and in southern Germany, central Germany, Moravia, the Netherlands, northern Europe, and Russia.

The initial movement was given shape by a gathering of leaders in Schleitheim, on the southern German border, in February 1527. Known as the Schleitheim Confession, these seven articles articulated the foundations of the new movement:

(1) Baptism—Baptism is for all who repent, undergo conversion, and practice discipleship.
(2) Ban—A ban will be used against Christians who fall into error and sin.
(3) Lord's Supper—Those who wish to share in this memorial shall be baptized members of Christ's church.
(4) Separation—Believers shall separate themselves from the evil of the world.
(5) Pastors—Pastors shall lead the church and see to its care. When executed, they shall be replaced quickly so that the congregation will be preserved.
(6) Sword—The sword is ordained of God outside the perfection of Christ.
(7) Oath—The swearing of oaths is forbidden.

Michael Sattler was likely the primary voice behind this document. He was executed, along with his wife, three months later.

The scattered movement gained a new unity in Holland under the leadership of Menno Simons. Ordained a Catholic priest in 1524, Simons identified himself with the peaceful Anabaptists of Holland in January 1536. The efforts of Menno Simons in the 1540s and 1550s saved the movement from fanaticism and violence and provided the leadership that insured its endurance. His followers became known as Menists or Mennonists and later as Mennonites. While a few Anabaptist congregations founded in the first decades of the movement remain, the Anabaptist tradition survives today in three major groups: Mennonites, Amish, and Hutterites.

The Sermon's Impact

Two convictions lie at the heart of Anabaptist thought and practice: (1) the Christian life is marked by conversion and discipleship, and (2) the church is a voluntary gathering of baptized believers separated from the world and the state. A major source for these convictions is the teaching of Jesus in the Sermon on the Mount.

For Anabaptists, discipleship is the central trait of a Christian life. Because of this, only believers who have willingly turned in faith to Christ should be baptized into the church. Key images for this theology of discipleship are drawn from the Sermon. In his farewell letter to his congregation at Horb, written a few days before his trial and execution, Michael Sattler urges his friends to "persevere in the discipline of your heavenly Father . . . that you might enter in through the gate."[2] The admonition not to resist evil is cited in the fourth article at Schleitheim. The command to practice nonviolence, found in the sixth article, and to refuse oaths, found in the seventh article, also reflect the impact of the Sermon. At his trial Sattler cited Matthew 5 to explain his rejection of oaths.[3] He presented an extended argument based on Matthew 5 in his essay, "On Two Kinds of Obedience."[4]

Thus, the idea of *nachfolge*, discipleship, dominated Anabaptist theology from the beginning. From this foundation emerges the integrity of Anabaptist thought. A Christian is one who turns to Christ in voluntary repentance. This act is symbolized through believer's baptism and confirmed through discipleship. Love of the enemy and nonviolence, drawn from the teachings of Jesus, characterize this discipleship. Such believers, when gathered in community, compose the church. Because the church is so defined, it cannot be identified with the world, and it cannot be encumbered by the interests of the state.

These values are remembered within the Anabaptist tradition through stories, particular through accounts of those who died for this faith. The story of Dirk Willems, recorded in *Martyrs Mirror*,[5] is often recalled. In 1569 Willems was pursued in Holland as a heretic. He escaped by fleeing across the thin ice covering a river. The thief-catcher who followed him could not negotiate the thin ice and fell into the river. Perceiving that the thief-catcher was in danger of death, Willems turned back and saved his life. Upon the insistence of the burgermeister standing on the shore, Willems was nonetheless arrested and taken away to prison. He was burned at the stake on May 16, 1569. Such stories embody the Anabaptist commitment to obey the teachings of Jesus.

The Continuing Impact

The Anabaptist tradition, an effort to restore a New Testament model based on the teachings of Jesus, continues today in a few Anabaptist congregations and in the traditions of the Mennonites, the Amish, and the Hutterites. These values are articulated in *Confession of Faith in a Mennonite Perspective*, a confession adopted jointly in 1995 by two North American groups, the Mennonite Church and the General Conference Mennonite Church.[6] This confession is framed around twenty-four articles, each followed by a short commentary, and it totals less than one hundred pages. Within this statement are some thirty-six references to the Sermon on the Mount (Matt 5–7) and two references to the Sermon on the Plain (Luke 6:17-49).

More importantly, these groups continue to embody a concept of discipleship deeply rooted in the ideals of the Sermon. Key traits characterize contemporary embodiments of the Anabaptist vision: Christian identity focused on voluntary conversion and baptism, discipleship as the defining trait of Christian identity, the church as a voluntary community of baptized believers, separation from state control, rejection of worldly values, the practice of a simple lifestyle, a witness to peace, the practice of nonviolence in the face of oppression, practical aid for the needy, and confidence in the Bible as a guide for faith and practice.

The history of the Anabaptists and modern attempts to implement the Anabaptist vision serve as important models. Here we find an authentic attempt to take seriously the teaching of Jesus and to realize, in a simple lifestyle of faith and obedience, the values of the Sermon on the Mount.

Dietrich Bonhoeffer
(1906–1945)

We turn now to a second model of how the Sermon on the Mount may be applied to human life. This model is found in the life of Dietrich Bonhoeffer, a Lutheran pastor who opposed Adolf Hitler and the Nazi movement.[7]

Life and Ministry

Dietrich Bonhoeffer was born in Germany in 1906. At the age of seventeen he entered the University of Tübingen to begin theological studies. After one year he began studies at the University of Berlin, from which he received his doctorate in theology. He studied from 1930 to 1931 at Union Theological Seminary in New York, where he came under the influence of Reinhold Niebuhr. During his theological studies he also was influenced by Adolf von Harnack at Berlin and by the writings of Karl Barth. After a year in Spain, Bonhoeffer began to lecture in systematic theology at the University of Berlin at the age of twenty-four.

Bonhoeffer spent his career as a Lutheran pastor, professor of theology, and worker in the ecumenical movement. By 1933 Bonhoeffer was resisting the growing influence of Nazism on the German churches. He associated himself with the Confessing Church, a group of Christians who separated from Lutheranism in order to oppose Hitler. After a brief pastorate in London, Bonhoeffer returned to Germany in 1935 to direct an illegal seminary where he prepared young pastors for ordination. Though he accepted an offer to teach at Union Theological Seminary in 1939, he returned quickly to Germany. "I shall have no right," Bonhoeffer wrote to his teacher, Reinhold Neibuhr, "to participate in the reconstruction of Christian life in Germany after the war if I do not share the trials of this time with my people."⁸

Bonhoeffer became actively involved in the opposition movement and took part in a plot to assassinate Hitler. In April 1943 he was arrested and imprisoned by the Gestapo. He continued his pastoral ministry among the prisoners, and from prison he continued to write. He was executed by special order of Himmler at Flossenburg on April 9, 1945, a few days before the camp was liberated.

The Sermon's Impact

Bonhoeffer leveled a scathing critique against the Christian church. His primary concern was what he saw as a sharp distinction between belief in the doctrines of Christianity and the practice of a Christlike way of life—the separation of faith from obedience.

From a theological perspective, Bonhoeffer raised this critique in the context of Luther's reformation of the Catholic Church. In Bonhoeffer's analysis, Luther saw that withdrawal into monastic life set up a double standard in which there existed a maximum and a minimum standard of obedience. Luther's abandonment of the monastery signified his recognition that true obedience was not the privilege of a cloistered few, but the obligation of all Christians. Thus, Luther returned to the world, seeking to live in full dependence upon God's grace. Luther understood that the extraordinary grace of God did not relieve Christians from the obligation to obedience; on the contrary, it was precisely God's grace that required obedience to Christ in the world. Bonhoeffer insisted the followers of Luther severed this connection between grace and discipleship: "The justification of the sinner in the world degenerated into the justification of sin and the world. Costly grace was turned into cheap grace without discipleship."⁹ For Bonhoeffer, this attraction to cheap grace threatened the existence of Christianity:

We confess that, although our Church is orthodox as far as her doctrine of grace is concerned, we are no longer sure that we are members of a Church which follows its Lord. We must therefore attempt to recover a true understanding of the mutual relation between grace and discipleship. The issue can no longer be evaded. It is becoming clearer every day that the most urgent problem besetting our Church is this: How can we live the Christian life in the modern world?[10]

From a practical perspective, Bonhoeffer expressed this critique through a term that became the German title of his book—*Nachfolge*, which means "discipleship." For Bonhoeffer, discipleship means simple, absolute obedience to Christ. This experience comes in the context of a community of believers, but it must be lived out in the world. Because discipleship means following Jesus in the world, it also means suffering and rejection and death.

Bonhoeffer found the primary foundation for this way of life in the Sermon on the Mount. He interpreted the Beatitudes of Matthew 5:1-12 as blessings already experienced by those who have answered the call of Jesus, thus becoming poor and hungry and oppressed.[11] For Bonhoeffer, the images of salt and light (5:13-16) present the disciple's mission to live in and for the whole earth.[12] The call to fulfill the Law (5:17-20) is obeyed only through following Jesus.[13] The Antitheses (5:21-48) represent a new way of life fulfilled in those who follow Christ.[14] In this manner Bonhoeffer interprets the Sermon as a call to discipleship—to active obedience in the way of Christ. The call of Jesus creates a separation between the church and the world, creates a dividing line that runs through the midst of the confessing church, and separates the confessor from the doer.[15] Thus, Dietrich Bonhoeffer found in the Sermon on the Mount the absolute unity of grace and obedience:

> Humanly speaking, we could understand and interpret the Sermon on the Mount in a thousand different ways. Jesus knows only one possibility: simple surrender and obedience, not interpreting it or applying it, but doing and obeying it. That is the only way to hear

his word. But again he does not mean that it is to be discussed as an ideal, he really means for us to get on with it. . . . The only proper response to this word which Jesus brings with him from eternity is simply to do it. Jesus has spoken: his is the word, ours is the obedience. Only in the doing of it does the word of Jesus retain its honour, might, and power among us.[16]

The Continuing Impact

The legacy of Dietrich Bonhoeffer presents an enigma. He expressed his patriotism by calling for the downfall of his nation. He expressed his love for the church through sharp critique. He called Christians to love their enemies while plotting the death of Hitler. His abiding legacy is found in his insistence that grace and discipleship, faith and practice, are inseparable and that righteousness comes not from pure doctrine, but from simple obedience to the call of Jesus. He envisioned the future of the church as a community, devoid of religiosity and self-interest, practicing radical discipleship in a secular world. Bonhoeffer's vision was shaped by the immediate crisis of his own age, but it was rooted in ancient ideals: the theological agenda of the Reformers and the biblical ideals of the Sermon.

Mahatma Gandhi
(1869–1948)

The third model seeking to actualize the values of the Sermon is found in the life of Mahatma Gandhi.[17] His profile is intriguing because he stood outside of the Christian tradition, yet he was deeply committed to the teachings of Jesus as he found them in the Sermon.

Life and Ministry

Gandhi was born in 1869 at Porbander, India, as Mohandas Karamchand Gandhi. As a sign of honor he was later given the title Mahatma, which means "The Great Soul in beggar's garb."[18] Gandhi entered an arranged marriage at the age of thirteen to Kasturbai Nakanji, a marriage that lasted sixty-two years.[19]

In 1888 Gandhi sailed for England to study law. By 1893 he was practicing law in South Africa. There he became an activist against the unfair treatment of Indians, organizing the Natal Congress. His first campaign of nonviolent resistance was carried out in Johannesburg in 1906. When Indians were required to register and carry certificates, Gandhi encouraged mass disobedience. He warned that this commitment would require patience and suffering. For this strategy he adopted the name *Satyagraha*. *Satya* means truth, and *Agraha* means force, with the resulting meaning of the force that is born of truth and love.[20]

This presentation of nonviolent resistance in the face of injustice provided the tool with which Gandhi would face the British Empire in India. Gandhi was jailed for his actions. He returned to India in 1914 and instigated his first campaign of nonviolent resistance in India by 1915. Gandhi also established an Ashram, or commune, which cut across the traditional caste system. His first comprehensive campaign of nonviolence was attempted for the whole of India in 1919. While others had advocated nonviolent resistance on an individual basis, Gandhi was the first to use it as a mass movement for social and political change.

From 1920 until his death in 1948, Gandhi carried out numerous campaigns of nonviolent resistance within India. Gandhi added to these mass movements other creative patterns of resistance. He use his numerous imprisonments to publicize his cause and to write. He carried out symbolic acts, for example, weaving his own cloth rather than buying it from the British and marching to the sea to make his own salt instead of purchasing it. These campaigns, along with other forces, pushed the British to grant independence to India in August 1947. This date was seen by Gandhi largely as a failure, for British India was partitioned into a Muslim Pakistan and a Hindu India. He felt that independence had been won at the cost of a value he held more important—the nonviolent force of truth and love.[21]

Gandhi spent the next five months traveling, fasting, and praying to calm the riots that resulted from the division of India. The agent of peace now stood at the center of the storm of violence. A bomb exploded in the midst of his prayer meeting on January 20, 1948. On January 30 he was assassinated at the age of seventy-eight. His final words were "Hey Rama" (O God).[22]

The Sermon's Impact

Gandhi's practice of nonviolent resistance shows affinities to Jesus' command to turn the other cheek in the face of violence. The idea came to Gandhi from a traditional Indian hymn, which began, "For a bowl of water give a goodly meal" and ends with "Return with gladness good for evil done."[23] While the idea came from this hymn, "it was the New Testament that fixed it in my heart," said Gandhi.[24] Though he never became a Christian, Gandhi expressed a deep connection to the person and the teaching of Jesus:

> I do not experience spiritual consciousness in my life through that Jesus (the historical Jesus). But if by Jesus you mean the eternal Jesus, if by Jesus you understand the religion of universal love that dwells in the heart, then that Jesus lives in my heart—to the same extent that Krishna lives, and that Rama lives.[25]

For Gandhi, the key to Jesus' teaching lies in the Sermon on the Mount. Gandhi said,

> The Sermon on the Mount went straight to my heart. The verses, "But I say unto you, That ye resist not evil: but whosoever shall smite thee on thy right cheek, turn to him the other also. And if any man . . . take away thy coat, let him have thy cloke also," delighted me beyond measure. . . . That renunciation was the highest form of religion appealed to me greatly.[26]

Gandhi was sometimes criticized for this view by other Hindu scholars, as is evident in this statement: "I must tell you that orthodox scholars have criticized my interpretation of the Gita as being unduly influenced by the Sermon on the Mount."[27] Because of his familiarity with the Sermon, Gandhi believed there was a vast chasm between the teachings of Jesus and the modern practice of Christianity:

> The message of Jesus, as I understand it, is contained in the Sermon on the Mount. . . . It is that Sermon which has endeared Jesus to me. . . . The message, to my mind, has suffered distortion in the West. . . . Much of what passes as Christianity is a negation of the Sermon on the Mount.[28]

The Continuing Impact

Mahatma Gandhi presents another enigmatic portrait. He was not a Christian, but he was deeply moved by the teachings of Jesus. He embraced Jesus but soundly criticized the western practice of Christianity. As a deeply religious Hindu, Gandhi attempted to actualize the power of nonviolent love in the face of injustice. He translated the command of Jesus into a mass social and political movement. Gandhi's thoughts and actions continue to raise the difficult question of whether the teachings of Jesus can be carried out in a non-Christian religious context. More importantly, they raise the difficult critique of whether a non-Christian (Gandhi) has proven more faithful to the teachings of Jesus than the church.

Martin Luther King, Jr.
(1929–1968)

Martin Luther King, Jr. sought to implement the teachings of Jesus within the American civil rights struggle of the 1950s and 1960s. His life integrates key movements and influences: Christian faith, Gandhian philosophy, African-American culture, American politics.[29]

Life and Ministry

Born in Atlanta in 1929, King entered Morehouse College at the age of fifteen. Following his graduation in 1948, King enrolled for theological studies at Crozer Theological Seminary in Pennsylvania. In 1955 he was awarded the Ph.D. in theology from Boston University. While there, he married Coretta Scott.

King chose to return to the South to carry out his ministry. He began his first pastorate at Dexter Avenue Baptist Church in Montgomery, Alabama, in 1954. Within a year of his arrival, Rosa Parks defied the city ordinance that required segregated seating on public buses. King's leadership in the Montgomery bus boycott brought him to the forefront of the civil rights movement. From this experience arose his first book, *Stride Towards Freedom*, published in 1958.

By 1960 King had resigned from Dexter Avenue Church and moved to Atlanta to assume the presidency of the Southern Christian Leadership Conference. King began to use nonviolent mass protests to publicize the movement, to interrupt unjust procedures, and to press for social and legal change. His numerous arrests and imprisonments brought a wider audience, and King continued to speak and to publish for the cause of civil rights.

The desegregation movement focused on Albany, Georgia, in 1961–1962, and then moved to the Birmingham campaign. Out of the Birmingham movement came further publications on the urgency of social reform: "Letter from Birmingham Jail" and *Why We Can't Wait*. Other campaigns were undertaken in Selma, Alabama, in Chicago, and in Mississippi. In 1963 King led the March on Washington for Jobs and Freedom. It was there that he delivered, before an audience of some 200,000, his famous "I Have a Dream" speech.

While various changes were underway throughout the country, the central impact of the civil rights movement was seen in the enactment of two pieces of federal legislation. In the wake of the assassination of John F. Kennedy, the Civil Rights Act was signed in 1964. The

Voting Rights Act followed in 1965. The power of the federal government now stood behind the movement for equality and civil rights.

By 1967 King was speaking out against the Vietnam War. In 1968 he sought to organize the Poor People's Campaign to Washington. Near the end of his life, he was seeking to create a unified national movement that would stop the war in Vietnam and replace it with a domestic program for social and economic reform.

In 1968, while organizing the Poor People's Campaign, King went to Memphis, Tennessee, to assist the striking garbage workers. While standing on the balcony of the Lorraine Motel, he was assassinated on April 4, 1968.

The Sermon's Impact

Martin Luther King, Jr. sought to confront the injustice and inequality of racial segregation through a variety of tools. He sought to publicize injustice by putting it on the front pages of American newspapers. He goaded the American legal system to enact the justice promised in its constitution and in its legal codes. He sought to expose the evil that was inherent in systems of segregation. He sought to encourage and energize the victims of racial hatred. He sought to disrupt the ability of unjust systems to suppress their victim. He traveled countless miles, and he preached and spoke and wrote in behalf of the movement.

The key tool in King's attack on racial segregation and economic and political injustice was his strategy of nonviolent resistance. Those who participated in his marches underwent careful instruction to insure that they did not strike back in the face of abuse or violence. King believed that nonviolent resistance was not only a personal stance, but also a powerful tool for social and political change. He believed that nonviolent resistance could interrupt and expose the power of injustice, but that it would also change the heart of the oppressor. In the tool of nonviolence King found a way to fight the enemy without succumbing to hatred and revenge.

King was clear on the source of his nonviolent strategy: "Christ furnished the spirit and motivation, and Gandhi furnished the method."[30] King's connection to Gandhi provided the intellectual foundation for nonviolence:

> As I delved into the philosophy of Gandhi, my skepticism concerning the power of love gradually diminished, and I came to see for the first time that the Christian doctrine of love, operating through the Gandhian method of nonviolence, is one of the most potent weapons available to an oppressed people in their struggle for freedom.[31]

King saw that this method was not only valid for relations between individuals, but also was valid on a mass scale. Eventually King saw the need for the method of nonviolence in international relations.[32]

The specific source for King's strategy of nonviolent resistance was the Sermon on the Mount. In a sermon entitled "Loving Your Enemies," King interpreted the command of Jesus from Matthew 5:43-45:

> Far from being the pious injunction of a utopian dreamer, the command to love one's enemy is an absolute necessity for our survival. Love even for enemies is the key to the solution of the problems of our world. Jesus is not an impractical idealist: he is the practical realist.[33]

King organized the sermon around two questions. To the question of "How do we love our enemies?" King insisted that one must develop and maintain the capacity to forgive. This does not mean ignoring what has been done, but it does mean no longer allowing the evil act to create a barrier in the relationship. One must also recognize that an evil act does not express the entire nature of a person. One must not seek to defeat or humiliate the enemy, but to win them over.[34]

To the question "Why should we love our enemies?" King answered that returning hate for hate only multiplies hate. Hating will scar the soul and distort the personality of the victim. Beyond this, love is the only force capable of transforming an enemy into a friend. Even more important than these reasons is the command to love enemies in order to act as God's children.[35]

King's understanding and application of the Sermon are to be found in the conclusion of this sermon:

> My friends, we have followed the so-called practical way for too long a time now, and it has led inexorably to deeper confusion and chaos. Time is cluttered with the wreckage of communities which surrendered to hatred and violence. For the salvation of our nation and the salvation of mankind, we must follow another way. This does not mean that we abandon our righteous efforts. With every ounce of our energy we must continue to rid this nation of the incubus of segregation. But we shall not in the process relinquish our privilege and our obligation to love. While abhorring segregation, we shall love the segregationist. This is the only way to create the beloved community.
>
> To our most bitter opponents we say: "We shall match your capacity to inflict suffering by our capacity to endure suffering. We shall meet your physical force with soul force. Do to us what you will, and we shall continue to love you. We cannot in all good conscience obey unjust laws, because non-cooperation with evil is as much a moral obligation as is cooperation with the good. Throw us in jail, and we shall still love you. Send your hooded perpetrators of violence into our communities and we shall still love you. But be ye assured that we will wear you down by our capacity to suffer. One day we shall win freedom, but not only for ourselves. We shall so appeal to your heart and conscience that we shall win *you* in the process, and our victory will be a double victory."[36]

The Continuing Impact

In the years following his death, King's program of nonviolent resistance was continued in the American civil rights movement, but it also impacted various movements for freedom throughout the world. A new South Africa, for example, is now seeking universal reconciliation by confronting the evil of its past and extending the offer of forgiveness to the instigators of violence. Beyond this the unique challenge of King lives on in his insistence that we find a way to bring the teachings of Jesus to bear upon the violence, oppression, and injustice of our own age.

Clarence Jordan
(1912–1969)

The fifth witness to the Sermon is found in the life of Clarence Jordan.[37] Clarence sought to realize the claims of the gospel by working for a community of equality in Georgia in the 1950s and 1960s.

Life and Ministry

Clarence Leonard Jordan was born in 1912 in Talbotton, Georgia. As a child he recognized the conflict between the religious values proclaimed in his community and the violent racial hatred practiced there. He considered the study of law, but went instead to the University of Georgia, in 1929, to study agriculture. He hoped to become a scientific farmer and to aid poor farmers. Upon his graduation from the university he did not turn immediately to farming, but enrolled instead at the Southern Baptist Theological Seminary in Louisville, Kentucky, There he met Florence Kroeger, and they were married in 1936. Jordan continued his study, pursuing a doctorate in the study of New Testament Greek. His academic studies were accompanied by life-changing experiences in ministry. Clarence taught and worked among the African American communities in the West End of Louisville. These experiences, along with his immersion in the New Testament, provided the platform for later years of ministry.

In 1942 Florence and Clarence Jordan, along with Martin and Mabel England, purchased a farm in Sumter County, Georgia. The name of *Koinonia Farm* was taken from the term for community or fellowship in the Greek New Testament. Koinonia was envisioned as a community that

> seeks to combine religious training with actual experience in community service. . . . Devoted to the proclamation of Jesus Christ and the application of his teachings, Koinonia Farm hopes to make a contribution to the lives of all those who suffer and are oppressed; who are bound by ignorance and sin; and who are desperately searching for a way in the wilderness. . . .[38]

The goals of racial reconciliation and ecological nurture were articulated before the land was purchased. The purpose of Koinonia was:

> To relate, through a ministry to both individuals and community, the entire life of the people to Jesus Christ and his teachings. To undertake to train Negro preachers in religion and agriculture. To provide an opportunity for Christian students to serve a period of apprenticeship in developing community life on the teachings and principles of Jesus. To seek to conserve the soil, which we believe to be God's holy earth. . . .[39]

These lofty ideals expressed in their founding documents did not suggest the difficulty and violence that would follow. Interracial Bible studies were initiated, and farming was begun. They began to offer housing and support for alcoholics and for draft resisters. Youth clubs were organized, and the farm began selling produce from roadside stands.

A new direction was taken in 1968 with the arrival of Millard and Linda Fuller. Having abandoned the wealth gained from their business, they went to the farm to restore their marriage and to seek a new direction for their lives. They brought new ideas and new impetus to Koinonia Farm. Through a strategy known as Koinonia Partners and the Fund for Humanity the farm planned to provide partnership industries, partnership farming, and partnership housing. The most dramatic of these ideas was partnership housing. Land was provided, houses were built and sold at cost, and purchasers were given interest-free loans for a period of twenty years. In this way Koinonia hoped to bring the dispossessed into home ownership. In addition to these activities, Clarence carried out a busy speaking schedule, wrote books and letters, and translated parts of the New Testament into folksy Southern dialect.

Throughout its history the active idealism of Koinonia Farm was met by violence from the surrounding community. In 1950 the Jordan family was "churched"; they were excommunicated from Rehoboth Baptist Church because of their racial views. The health department closed their summer camps in 1956, and the local community began a boycott of Koinonia products that lasted into the 1960s. Their produce stands were bombed, shots were fired into their homes, grand juries were convened against them, and the Ku Klux Klan appeared on the farm to threaten violence. The business of a local merchant who sold to Koinonia was bombed in 1957, and in 1960 residents had to sue to have their children admitted to public schools.

Clarence and other members of Koinonia responded to the violence and rejection in prophetic and creative ways. Clarence challenged the Baptists with the Bible they so loved. When the motion for their dismissal from the church was read, Florence Jordan stood to move for its approval. Clarence wrote creative paraphrases of New Testament parables that spoke to the injustice around them. Koinonia residents continued to sell their products, but through mail-order services.

In 1969, at the age of fifty-seven, Clarence died from cardiac arrest. The coroner refused to go to the farm to pronounce him dead, so Clarence was taken into town in a van. He was buried in a wooden crate in an unmarked grave on Koinonia Farm.

The Sermon's Impact

The creative social activism of Clarence Jordan was shaped by many influences: his experience with racism as a youth, his love of the land, his theological education, his inner-city ministry experience, and the many colleagues who shared his life. The key to his experience, however, was a radical commitment to practice the teachings of Jesus. For these, Clarence turned to the Sermon on the Mount. Apart from his translations, his commentary on the Sermon was the place where his practical theology passed into writing.[40] Clarence found in the words of the Sermon the call to the Kingdom of God. His interpretation of the command to love one's enemies (5:38-44) typifies Jordan's understanding of the Sermon.

> It is with this kingdom that the Sermon on the Mount concerns itself. We shall be better prepared to understand this great discourse of the Master's if, before entering upon a study of it, we keep constantly before us certain things about the kingdom.[41]
>
> . . . .
>
> Here Jesus is simply saying that, for kingdom citizens, love must be the basis of all relationships and that it must be applied universally, both to one's race and nation and to those of other races and nations. There must be no double-dealing, no two-facedness, no partiality. Hate has the same effect upon the personality whether its object is friend or foe. Spiritual traffic cannot be halted at the artificial borders of caste or nation.[42]

Jordan's life experience is reflected in his evaluation of this commitment to unlimited love.

> The truth is that in its initial stages unlimited love is very impractical. Folks who are determined enough to hold on to it usually wind up on a cross, like Jesus. Their goods get plundered, and they get slandered. Persecution is their lot. Surely nobody would be inclined to call this practical. Yet in its final stages unlimited love seems to be the only thing that can possibly make any sense.[43]

The Continuing Impact

The impact of Clarence Jordan's life survives in several forums. Because of his early death, the memory and stories of Clarence live on with his friends and colleagues. Through his writings and recordings subsequent generations are still confronted by the folksy prophetic voice of Jordan. Koinonia Partners continues to operate on a small scale. Perhaps the most enduring legacy of Jordan is to be found elsewhere. Some 192 houses were built by Koinonia Partners from 1969 to1992. Through the efforts of Rosalyn and Jimmy Carter, natives of nearby Plains, Georgia, the commitment to build affordable housing for the poor was widely publicized. Working in every state in the U.S. and in more than 60 countries, Habitat for Humanity has built more than 70,000 homes. In such acts of faith Clarence Jordan's vision of the Sermon on the Mount lives on.

Chris Carrier

The final model for how the values of the Sermon may be realized in new and changing contexts comes from contemporary life. This report appeared in newspapers a few years ago:

> David McAllister, 77 and blind, a nursing-home invalid in North Miami Beach, Fla., receives daily visits from Chris Carrier, 32, who reads to McAllister from the Bible. Their only previous relationship occurred during a few days in December 1974, when McAllister kidnapped young Carrier at a bus stop and left him for dead in the Everglades with cigarette burns on his body, ice-pick holes in one eye, and a gunshot wound that left him blind in the other eye.

Carrier, now grown, reflected upon this experience in an article entitled "Full Circle: The Power of Forgiveness." Following is a summary of his story:

When Chris regained consciousness six days after the assault, he was unaware that he had been shot. He sat by the side of the road until a man stopped to help him. The assault left Chris blind in his left eye, but otherwise he was uninjured. With the love and support of his family and friends, he returned to school and resumed a normal life.

For the next three years Chris lived with tremendous anxiety. Most nights he would wake up frightened, imagining he heard someone coming in the back door, so he would sleep at the foot of his parents' bed. But when he was thirteen, he experienced a major change in his life. He recounts: "One night, during a Bible study with my church youth group, I realized that God's providence and love, having miraculously kept me alive, were the basis for my life's security. In His hands, I could live without fear or anger. And so I did."

Chris finished high school, earned a bachelor's and a master of divinity degree, and married a young lady named Leslie. He and his wife now have two young daughters, Amanda and Melodee.

A most interesting change of events in Carrier's life took place in September 1996. Major Charles Scherer of the Coral Gables Police Department, who had worked on the original investigation of Chris' case, called to tell him that 77-year-old David McAllister had confessed to the assault. Blind from glaucoma, in poor health, without family or friends, McAllister was living in a North Miami Beach nursing home.

Chris felt the need to visit his assailant. He recalls the forgiveness and peace they both experienced:

> The first time I went to see him, he apologized for what he had done to me, and I told him that I had forgiven him. I visited him many times after that, introducing him to my wife and girls, offering him hope and some semblance of family in the days before his death. He was always glad when I came by. I believe that our friendship eased his loneliness and was a great relief to him after 22 years of regrets.
>
> I know the world might view me as a victim of a horrible tragedy, but I consider myself the "victim" of many miracles. The fact that I'm alive and have no mental deficiencies defies the odds. I've got a loving wife and a beautiful family. I've been given as much promise as anybody else, and ample opportunities. I've been blessed in a lot of ways.
>
> And while many people can't understand how I could forgive David McAllister, from my point of view I couldn't *not* forgive him.

If I'd chosen to hate him all these years, or spent my life looking for revenge, then I wouldn't be the man I am today, the man my wife and children love.[44]

Chris Carrier is not a well-known personality like Dietrich Bonhoeffer, Mahatma Gandhi, Martin Luther King, and Clarence Jordan, but he too has been impacted deeply by the teachings of Jesus in the Sermon on the Mount. Each of these men, along with their ancestors, the Anabaptists, is a model of how individual Christians can and should apply the teachings of the Sermon in their lives.

Notes

[1] For a helpful summary of Anabaptist origins and development, see William R. Estep, *The Anabaptist Story* (Nashville: Broadman Press, 1975); Cornelius J. Dyck, *An Introduction to Mennonite History: A Popular History of the Anabaptists and the Mennonites*, 3d ed. (Scottdale PA: Herald Press, 1993); Donald F. Durnbaugh, *The Believers' Church: The History and Character of Radical Protestantism* (Scottdale PA: Herald Press, 1965, 1985).

[2] Cited in *The Legacy of Michael Sattler*, tr. and ed. John H. Yoder (Scottsdale PA: Herald Press, 1973) 62.

[3] Cited in Yoder, 72.

[4] Cited in Yoder, 123.

[5] *Martyrs Mirror* is a compilation of martyr stories from the time of Christ until 1660, compiled in Dutch in 1660 by Thieleman J. Braght. For the story of Dirk Willem, see the 1996 edition (Scottdale PA: Herald Press) 741-42.

[6] Herald Press, Scottdale PA.

[7] For an overview of Bonhoeffer's life, see Eberhard Bethge, "Dietrich Bonhoeffer," in *The Encyclopedia of Religion*, ed. Mircea Eliade, vol. 2 (New York: MacMillan, 1987) 285-87; the memoir by G. Leibholz, which serves as a preface to Bonhoeffer's *The Cost of Discipleship* (New York: Simon and Schuster, 1995) 14-33.

[8] Cited in by G. Leibholz in the preface to *The Cost of Discipleship*, 18.

[9] Bonhoeffer, 50.

[10] Ibid., 55.

¹¹Ibid., 105-14.
¹²Ibid., 115-19.
¹³Ibid., 120-25.
¹⁴Ibid., 154.
¹⁵Ibid., 189-95.
¹⁶Ibid., 196-97.
¹⁷Helpful for the study of Gandhi's life and message are the following: *The Gandhi Reader: A Source Book of His Life and Writings*, ed. Homer A. Jack (Bloomington: Indiana University Press, 1956); Louis Fischer, *The Life of Mahatma Gandhi* (New York: Harper and Row, 1950, 1983); *Gandhi: All Men Are Brothers*, ed. Krishna Kripalani (New York: Continuum, 1982); Erik H. Erikson, *Gandhi's Truth: On the Origins of Militant Nonviolence* (New York: W. W. Norton, 1969); Margaret Chatterjee, *Gandhi's Religious Thought* (Notre Dame: University of Notre Dame Press, 1983).
¹⁸Fischer, 128.
¹⁹Ibid., 16.
²⁰*The Gandhi Reader*, 65.
²¹Fischer, 473-75.
²²*The Gandhi Reader*, 475.
²³E. Stanley Jones, *Mahatma Gandhi: An Interpretation* (New York: Abingdon-Cokesbury, 1948) 82.
²⁴Jones, 82.
²⁵Cited in Chatterjee, 53.
²⁶Jones, 83.
²⁷*The Gandhi Reader*, 469.
²⁸Cited in Pinchas Lapide, *The Sermon on the Mount: Utopia or Program for Action?* trans. A. Swidler (Maryknoll NY: Orbis Books, 1986 [1982]) 3.
²⁹For a biographical sketch of King's life, see the article by David Levering Lewis in *Dictionary of American Negro Biography*, ed. Rayford Logan and Michael Winston (New York: W. W. Norton, 1982) 376-79. Representative sermons from King may be found in his book *Strength to Love* (Philadelphia: Fortress Press, 1981). For a collection of King's writings, see *A Testament of Hope: The Essential Writings of Martin Luther King, Jr.*, ed. James M. Washington (San Francisco: Harper and Row, 1986).
³⁰King, 150.
³¹Ibid.
³²King, 151.
³³King, 49-50.

[34]King, 50-52.
[35]King, 52-56.
[36]King, 56.
[37]For a portrait of Jordan's life, see Dallas Lee, *The Cotton Patch Evidence* (New York: Harper & Row, 1971). Information on Koinonia Farms is available on the internet at <www.koinoniapartners.org.>
[38]Lee, 32.
[39]Ibid.
[40]Clarence Jordan, *Sermon on the Mount*, rev. ed. (Valley Forge PA: Judson Press, 1993).
[41]Jordan, 4-5.
[42]Jordan, 45-48.
[43]Jordan, 48.
[44]Chris Carrier, "Full Circle: The Power of Forgiveness," in *Family Circle* (22 April 1997) 162.

Epilogue

The Gospel of Matthew represents an attempt to live out the teachings of Jesus in the context of a Jewish Christian community sometime after 70 CE, in the aftermath of the fall of the Jerusalem Temple. The early church took the teachings of Jesus into new places and times; there they struggled to find the meaning of his message for their situation. The Anabaptists sought to live out the teachings of Jesus amidst the changing tides of sixteenth-century Europe. Faced with the growing power of Hitler and National Socialism, Dietrich Bonhoeffer led the Confessing Church of Germany in its protest. Mahatma Gandhi found in the teachings of Jesus the key to nonviolent resistance, and he turned this movement toward justice and liberation for India. Martin Luther King, Jr., adopted Jesus' message and Gandhi's method to lead the struggle for civil rights in the United States. Clarence Jordan sought to follow Jesus by preaching and farming and building a community in South Georgia. Chris Carrier teaches his children, through his example, that love and forgiveness are greater than hate.

Each of these, and so many others, sought to live out the values of the Sermon in the context of their own time and place. We do well to learn from them. But we cannot follow Jesus as members of a first-century community. We cannot join the Anabaptists or share Bonhoeffer's struggles. We cannot sit with Gandhi or march with King. If we are to live out the values of the Sermon, if we are to follow Jesus, we must do so in our own time, in our own places. This is no simple task. If the Sermon is to remain relevant it must be translated and interpreted into the language of the people; it must be addressed to the questions and needs of our lives; it must speak to our hearts and call us to action in our world. Otherwise, the Sermon remains an ancient text in a foreign language addressed to the concerns of another age.

At the same time the Sermon is not another tool to be manipulated in the search for meaning. Its values and power cannot be domesticated either by the church or the world. The Sermon is ultimately not a packet of information or a collection of unchanging doctrine. It is, instead, a timeless call to obedience in the way of Jesus. It is a call to faith and service in the Kingdom of God. It is a call to life.

Annotated Bibliography

Contemporary Issues/Sermon on the Mount

Bonhoeffer, D. *The Cost of Discipleship.* New York: MacMillan, 1963. A classic work by a German pastor from the time of World War II, this book issues a call for a Christianity marked by obedience to Jesus.

Davenport, G. *Into the Darkness: Discipleship in the Sermon on the Mount.* Nashville: Abingdon Press, 1988. A careful reading of the Sermon that gives sharp focus to the demands of contemporary discipleship.

Gill, A. *Life on the Road: The Gospel Basis for a Messianic Lifestyle.* Homebush West, New South Wales: Lancer, 1989. A provocative series of studies on discipleship.

_____ *The Fringes of Freedom: Following Jesus, Living Together, Working for Justice.* Homebush West, New South Wales: Lancer, 1990. A collection of essays on Christian lifestyles.

Jordan, C. *Sermon on the Mount.* Valley Forge PA: Judson Press, 1974. A prophetic reading of the Sermon in light of contemporary issues of the 1960s and 1970s.

King, M. L. Jr. *Why We Can't Wait.* New York: Signet Books, 1964. A series of essays in which Martin Luther King, Jr., who was greatly influenced by the Sermon, explains the ideas and strategies behind the civil rights movement.

Lapide, P. *The Sermon on the Mount: Utopia or Program for Action?* Maryknoll NY: Orbis, 1986/1982. A Jewish scholar seeks to demonstrate the relevance of the Sermon for social issues.

Thielicke, H. *Life Can Begin Again: Sermons on the Sermon on the Mount.* Philadelphia: Fortress Press, 1963/1956. A helpful collection by a German scholar.

Ethics of Jesus

Manson, T.W. *Ethics and the Gospel.* London: SCM, 1960. Gives focus to the ethic of suffering and service embraced by Jesus and the early church.

Wilder, A. *Eschatology and Ethics in the Teaching of Jesus*, 2d. ed. New York: Harper, 1950. Gives focus to the immediate ethical relevance of Jesus' teachings.

Gospel of Matthew

Broadus, J. *The Gospel of Matthew.* Philadelphia: The American Baptist Publication Society, 1886. A valuable treatment representative of the piety and scholarship of an earlier generation.

Garland, D. *Reading Matthew: A Literary and Theological Commentary on the First Gospel.* London: SPCK, 1993. Focus is given primarily to the message of Matthew's Gospel.

Gundry, R. *Matthew: A Commentary on His Literary and Theological Art.* Grand Rapids: Eerdmans, 1982. A detailed analysis that seeks to shed light on early Christian handling of the Jesus tradition.

Kingsbury, J. *Matthew: A Commentary for Preachers and Others.* London: SPCK, 1978. Seeks to promote practical use of scholarly research.

Minear, P. *Matthew: The Teacher's Gospel.* London: Darton, Longman, & Todd, 1984. Gives focus to the structure of Matthew's Gospel and to its use in the early church.

Senior, D. *Invitation to Matthew: A Commentary on the Gospel of Matthew with Complete Text from the Jerusalem Bible.* Garden City NY: Image Books, 1977. Careful interpretation from a Catholic perspective.

Schweizer, E. *The Gospel According to Matthew.* London: SPCK, 1976. From a leading European scholar, with particular concern for Matthew's message.

Stagg, F. "Matthew." In *Broadman Bible Commentary*. Edited by C. Allen. Nashville: Broadman, 1969. A scholarly treatment with a consistent concern for piety and practice.

Luz, U. *Matthew: A Continental Commentary*. Minneapolis: Fortress Press, 1992. The best level of German-speaking scholarship in accessible form. Noted for its attention to both exegesis and the later effect of texts.

Kingdom of God

Beasley-Murray, G. *Jesus and the Kingdom of God*. Grand Rapids: Eerdmans, 1986. A careful study that argues the Kingdom of God began with Jesus but awaits future consummation.

Ladd, G. *Jesus and the Kingdom of God*. New York: Harper & Row, 1964. Argues for a view of the Kingdom that is both realized and futuristic.

Perrin, N. *The Kingdom of God in the Teaching of Jesus*. Philadelphia: Westminster, 1963. Includes a review of the history of scholarship on this issue. Considers the existential relevance of the Kingdom.

Schnackenburg, R. *God's Rule and Kingdom*. New York: Herder & Herder, 1963/1959. Argues that the Kingdom of God occupies a central role in Jesus' proclamation. While this Kingdom has futuristic aspects, it also demands a response in the present.

Sermon on the Mount

Bauman, C. *The Sermon on the Mount: A Modern Quest for Its Meaning*. Macon GA: Mercer University Press, 1985. Surveys major studies on the Sermon and provides bibliographical information.

Betz, H. D. *Essays on the Sermon on the Mount*. Philadelphia: Fortress, 1985. Sees the Sermon as a pre-Matthean presentation of Jesus' teaching.

Donaldson, T. *Jesus on the Mountain: A Study in Matthean Theology*. Sheffield: JSOT, 1985. Compares the Sermon to other "mountain" stories in the Gospel of Matthew.

Davies, W. D. *The Setting of the Sermon on the Mount*. Cambridge: University Press, 1964. An influential work that seeks to show that the Sermon provides an accurate reflection of Jesus' own teaching.

Friedlander, G. *The Jewish Sources of the Sermon on the Mount*. New York: Bloch, 1911, 1969. Deals with both the original sermon by Jesus and its later use by early Christians.

Guelich, R. *The Sermon on the Mount: A Foundation for Understanding*. Waco TX: Word, 1982. Argues that Matthew presents the Sermon by employing materials that go back to Jesus.

Hunter, A. *Design for Life: An Exposition of the Sermon on the Mount, Its Making, Its Exegesis, and Its Meaning*. London: SCM, 1953. A useful exposition designed for a wider audience.

Jeremias, J. *The Sermon on the Mount*. Philadelphia: Fortress, 1963/1959. A careful analysis by a German scholar, with particular focus given to the role of the Sermon in early Christianity.

Kissinger, W. *The Sermon on the Mount: A History of Interpretation and Bibliography*. Metuchen: American Theological Library Association, 1975. A helpful bibliography and overview of the history of research on the Sermon.

Lambrecht, J. *The Sermon on the Mount: Proclamation and Exhortation*. Wilmington DE: Glazier, 1985/1983. Seeks to demonstrate the central role of Jesus' teaching behind Matthew's presentation of the Sermon.

Strecker, G. *The Sermon on the Mount: An Exegetical Commentary*. Edinburgh: T&T Clark, 1988/1985. Detailed exegetical treatment that seeks to show that the core of the Sermon goes back to Jesus.

Windisch, H. *The Meaning of the Sermon on the Mount.* Philadelphia: Westminster, 1951. An influential work that seeks to show how Jesus, as an orthodox Jew, would interpret God's Law.

www.ingramcontent.com/pod-product-compliance
Lightning Source LLC
Chambersburg PA
CBHW061447040426
42450CB00007B/1257